WOMEN IN THE CHURCH'S MINISTRY:

A Test-case for Biblical Hermeneutics

R. T. FRANCE
Principal of Wycliffe Hall, Oxford

Wipf & Stock
PUBLISHERS
Eugene, Oregon

Wipf and Stock Publishers
199 West 8th Avenue, Suite 3
Eugene, Oregon 97401

Women in the Church's Ministry
A Test-Case for Biblical Hermeneutics
By France, R.T.
Copyright©1995 Paternoster Press
ISBN: 1-59244-617-5
Publication date 4/20/2004
Previously published by Paternoster Press, 1995

This Edition reprinted by Wipf and Stock Publishers
by arrangement with Paternoster Press

Paternoster
9 Holdom Avenue
Bletchley
Milton Keyes, MK1 1QR
PATERNOSTER Great Britain

WOMEN IN THE CHURCH'S MINISTRY:

A Test-case for Biblical Hermeneutics

THE DIDSBURY LECTURES 1995

The Didsbury Lectures are delivered annually
at the Nazarene Theological College, Manchester
by leading scholars from a variety of schools of thought

Lecturers have included James Atkinson, C. K. Barrett,
Paul Bassett, F. F. Bruce, Ronald E. Clements,
David J. A. Clines, Alex R. G. Deasley,
James D. G. Dunn, R. T. France, Colin E. Gunton,
Donald Guthrie, Morna D. Hooker, I. Howard Marhall,
A. Skevington-Wood, James B. Torrance,
Thomas F. Torrance, and Andrew F. Walls

Contents

TO MY COLLEAGUES AND STUDENTS
AT
WYCLIFFE HALL
1989 – 1995
who have helped me to think through
the issues discussed in this book,
and to see why they matter.

Preface

The invitation, late in 1991, to deliver the 1995 Didsbury Lectures came with the generous licence to lecture on any subject of my choice, though with the expectation that it would be in the area of New Testament studies. During the years which have followed the initial invitation one of the most pressing issues, for one engaged in training those called to ordained ministry in the Church of England, has been the ordination of women. As the new situation has developed it has become increasingly clear to me that the differing positions which are held on this issue, particularly among evangelical Anglicans, raise interesting and important questions of biblical interpretation, and the approaching Didsbury Lectures offered an opportunity to explore these questions which I could not resist. I am grateful to the Principal of the Nazarene Theological College for encouraging me to indulge my perhaps rather parochial interests in this way, and to the audience of the lectures for bearing with me.

I dare to hope that the issues raised, even if they do not have the same specific relevance outside Church of England circles, will be found to apply much more widely in principle. Whatever the particular points of debate within Anglicanism, the broader question of how men and women relate to one another in the ministry of the church is one which will not only continue to be important in the wider church scene but which even outside the church walls has gained a new level of interest in a British society which has recently taken the Vicar of Dibley to its heart! The focus of this book is on the discussion of the issue in evangelical circles, where appeal is made instinctively to the authority of Scripture, so that the co-existence of opposite views each claiming to be based on the Bible has a peculiarly uncomfortable feel. But of course evangelicals have no monopoly on the use of the Bible as a guide to the thinking and life of the church, and I hope that Christians of all persuasions will find in these lectures some stimulus towards thinking out what it means to claim that our theology and practice is 'biblical'.

Because the question is of topical relevance, I have taken the unusual step of requesting the Paternoster Press, who traditionally publish the Didsbury Lectures after the event, to have this book ready for publication at the time the lectures are given. I am grateful for the eager cooperation of the Press in this. The lectures are therefore offered here in the form in which they are to be delivered, with only a little annotation and adaptation to the printed page.

The book is dedicated to my colleagues and students at Wycliffe Hall, past and present, in whose company I have been able to develop my own thinking in this sensitive area. Not all of them will agree with what I have written, but I hope that they and other readers will recognise my sincerity in trying to help those who find themselves divided on the issue to be able to understand and respect one another's positions, and so to continue to work together in harmony in the ministry of the gospel which is so much bigger and more vital than the issues which divide us.

My thanks especially to my colleagues Vera Sinton and David Wenham for valuable comments on the first draft of these lectures, which have saved me from some unnecessary misunderstandings.

Dick France
Christmas 1994

CHAPTER ONE

Opposite Conclusions from the Same Bible:

How Can This Be?

Setting the scene

On 11th November 1992 the General Synod of the Church of England reached the end of a long process of decision-making when it voted by a majority of more than two to one to approve the ordination of women to the office of priest (or 'presbyter').[1] The decision was made that day, and has since been implemented with the ordination of more than a thousand women priests, but the debate has gone on. While some of those who opposed the decision have left the Church of England, most of them remain within its structure, but as a self-consciously distinct group (or rather groups) who continue to refuse to have anything to do with women priests and, as far as is practically possible, with those who have ordained them.

Those who have opposed the Synod's decision have done so, generally, on theological grounds. They believe that, whatever may be acceptable in society at large, within the church it is not appropriate for women to hold

---

1 While 'priest' has been the term most used in the discussion, and is the term used in the official formularies of the Church of England, many evangelicals prefer to use the term 'presbyter' (from which 'priest' is etymologically derived) so as to avoid the more sacerdotal associations with which the more catholic members of the church invest the term 'priest'. While this usage is generally intelligible (if surprising to those used to the traditional term) within the Church of England, it can cause confusion in discussion with members of other churches which use 'elder' (presbyter) to denote officers other than ordained ministers. I shall discuss the nature of 'priesthood' in the modern Church of England more fully in the next chapter, but for the purposes of this discussion I shall stick to the term 'priest', as the accepted terminology, while sharing the misgivings of other evangelicals as to the implications it is sometimes made to carry.

the office of priest, and that the church must resist the tendency in society to eliminate any distinction between the roles appropriate to men and to women.

They are, however, by no means united on the basis for this resistance. Those on the catholic wing of the Church of England base their opposition on the continuity of the tradition of the church since the time of the (all male) apostles, on the contention that while the Roman Catholic and Orthodox churches remain unable to approve such a step the Church of England (together with its Anglican partners in other parts of the world, several of whom have been ordaining women as priests for many years)[2] has no right to make such a decision unilaterally, and on the belief that it is 'ontologically' impossible for a woman to be a priest since Christ was a man, and the priest represents Christ at the altar.[3]

But others who oppose the decision are evangelicals, to whom these catholic arguments are at best unpersuasive and at worst bizarre. For them the issue is simple: Scripture is the ultimate guide to faith and practice; Scripture teaches that women should not teach or hold authority over men; the role of an Anglican priest is one of teaching and authority; and therefore women may not hold the office of priest. The decision of the General Synod is, for them, a simple rejection of the plain teaching of Scripture. It is with their position that this book will be concerned.

The purpose of this book

At this point, I must offer a word of explanation as to why I am focusing on the internal debates of the Church of England in a series of lectures delivered in a non-Anglican context. I understand that the Church of the Nazarene, whose college sponsors these lectures, has had women in ordained ministry throughout its history, so you may well wonder what the fuss is about, and why I should expect you to have any interest in the benighted scruples of some

---

2 The first Anglican ordination of a woman priest took place in Hong Kong as long ago as 1944.
3 It is, of course, just this sort of theology which makes some evangelicals uneasy over the continued use of the word 'priest'.

of your Anglican colleagues! But my concern is not primarily with church structures as such, but with the theological issues which are uncovered when proposals are made to alter them. I hope that the issues concerning biblical interpretation which I shall put before you will be found to have relevance far beyond the specific issue of the ordination of women to Anglican priesthood. And I dare hazard a guess that even in a church where the ordination of women as such is not an issue, the relative role of men and women in ministry, and the extent to which the church can and should conform to the expectations of an equal opportunity society, may still have some practical relevance.

The reason why I dare to ask you to consider our Anglican debate, or rather more specifically the debate which has arisen over this issue within the evangelical part of the Church of England, is that I have become increasingly aware that it has raised fundamental questions of hermeneutical method which have hitherto tended to be ignored. Where such issues are left unaddressed, as is still too often the case, the resulting lack of methodological awareness has clouded discussion to the extent that those taking different sides hardly hear what the other is saying, while totally opposite conclusions are drawn from the same Bible, and each side is convinced that they alone have 'got it right'. Too easily this polarisation of views degenerates into mutual suspicion, and into accusations on the one side of unthinking fundamentalism and on the other of having surrendered the authority of Scripture under the pressure of the all-conquering liberal agenda of society and of those in the church who prefer conformity to confrontation. What both sides find hard to accept is that the opposing conclusions might in fact have been honestly reached by people of equal integrity and equal commitment to the authority of Scripture, who are divided not by incompatible theological starting-points, but by differing perceptions of the nature of the hermeneutical enterprise, of the fundamental question of how we get from an authoritative ancient text to the responsible application of biblical principles in the modern world.

While the specific focus of this book is on the issue of women's ministry, therefore, and I hope to be able to say some useful things on that subject, the 'real' subject is biblical hermeneutics, an area of which the importance has come to be widely recognised, at least in our evangelical Anglican circles, only within the last twenty years. Before that, while there were plenty of good evangelical text-books on the interpretation of the Bible, they tended to focus primarily on the exegetical task (grasping the meaning of the text in its original context) rather than on the far more difficult issue of how to get from 'what it meant' to 'what it means'. The latter enterprise was by and large assumed to operate on self-evident lines; once the text was properly understood in itself, its application to modern issues would follow almost automatically. At any rate, there were well-established conventions (largely unconscious) as to how Scripture should be applied to contemporary issues, and as long as one operated within the circle of those who shared these conventions the task was relatively painless. Others, primarily non-evangelicals, who disagreed with the conventional interpretations were easily dismissed as not serious in their claim to accept the authority of Scripture, and therefore of no account for 'Bible-believing' Christians beyond constituting the 'enemy' to be refuted and opposed.

Already in the nineteen-seventies this cosy world of illusion was beginning to look less secure. For evangelical Anglicans the moment of truth was the second National Evangelical Anglican Congress, held at Nottingham in 1977, when the hermeneutical issue was placed squarely on the table especially by Dr Anthony Thiselton, whose writings on the subject have continued to be at the cutting edge of discussion ever since.[4] However erudite and inaccessible to the ordinary church member some of the discussion may have seemed, it has been impossible since then to be unaware that old certainties might not always be well grounded, and that even among equally committed evangelicals there is room for debate and disagree-

---

4 A.C. Thiselton, 'Understanding God's Word Today', in J.R.W. Stott (ed.), *Obeying Christ in a Changing World: 1. The Lord Christ* (London: Collins, 1977) 90–122 (one of the three preparatory books for the Congress). Cf his articles 'Semantics and NT Interpretation' and 'The New Hermeneutic' in I.H. Marshall (ed.), *New Testament Interpretation* (Exeter: Paternoster ,1977) 75–104, 308–333. His major contributions since then have been *The Two Horizons* (Exeter: Paternoster, 1980) and *New Horizons in Hermeneutics* (London: Harper Collins, 1992).

ment as to how biblical texts should be applied to issues of modern church life and thought. But while some have welcomed this new openness with relief and optimism, others have felt profoundly threatened, and have tended to retreat into a reaffirmation of traditional evangelical patterns of thought which has in effect ruled the hermeneutical debate out of court. The authority of the evangelical tradition has too often, in practice if not in theory, taken precedence over the authority of Scripture.

The debate over the ordination of women to the priesthood has brought these issues more clearly into the open, and thus offers us the opportunity to analyse why and how it is that evangelicals can come to opposite conclusions from the same Bible. That is the aim of this book.

Authority and interpretation

What unites all evangelicals, and indeed constitutes probably the most generally recognised definition of what it is to be evangelical, is a conviction that the Scriptures of the Old and New Testaments, being of divine origin, have 'supreme authority in all matters of faith and conduct'.[5] In what follows I hope I may be allowed to take these fundamental evangelical convictions, of the divine origin and authority of the Bible, as given. In so far as this book is devoted to discussing the debate between evangelicals, this doctrine of Scripture, which would be agreed by all concerned, need not be put in question.

The fundamental evangelical conviction of the authority of Scripture has, however, sometimes been supported by two further assumptions, which have been conveniently summarised as the 'sufficiency' and the 'perspicuity' of Scripture. It is these two latter slogans, rather than the fundamental claim to authority, which have become the focus of debate among evangelicals in the light of recent hermeneutical questions.

By the 'sufficiency' of Scripture is generally understood the belief that all we need for our Christian belief and life

---

5 These words, from the Doctrinal Basis of the Universities and Colleges Christian Fellowship, a widely-respected statement of evangelical belief, would be agreed by most evangelicals.

is contained in Scripture, at least in principle. Clearly there are countless specific issues in modern life and thought on which Scripture is silent, if what is desired is a directly applicable quotation. But the intelligent use of principles derived from Scripture should, on this view, be sufficient to leave us in no doubt as to the will of God in our new, and varying, situations. We need not look elsewhere.

By the 'perspicuity' of Scripture is meant a clarity such that an unbiased interpreter should be able to understand what is written sufficiently to be able to submit appropriately to its authority. This is not, presumably, to deny the presence in the Bible of obscure passages and ambiguous terminology, but to claim that, taken as a whole, Scripture will not mislead those who search there for God's truth and direction for living.

These two principles, reflecting the Reformation ideal of restoring the Bible to the possession and use of the faithful without need for an authorised interpreter, and thus providing them with reliable guidance for thought and life, have been widely approved, and in practice treated as self-evident, by evangelicals. It is thus inevitably disconcerting to find equally well-motivated Christians coming to conflicting conclusions from the same 'sufficient' and 'perspicuous' Bible, and even more so to hear some of them arguing that what has hitherto been accepted as the 'plain meaning' of Scripture can no longer be taken as a reliable pointer to the will of God for our generation. If 'Scripture says' that women must be silent in the churches, how can those who claim to live by its authority applaud the ordination of women to the priesthood?

In fact, of course, this is by no means an unfamiliar situation. Evangelical disagreement is a fact of life with which we all grew up. The alternative (and mutually exclusive) views and practices with regard to the mode and subjects of baptism, and the contrasting theologies of baptism which underlie them, have always been defended vigorously by both sides as the clear teaching of Scripture on the subject. The same Scripture has allowed equally devout evangelicals to reach sharply opposed views on creation and evolution, war and pacifism, systems of church government, political agendas, millennial schemes, the nature of 'eternal punishment', and many other issues. Nor are these minor issues on which one may comfortably agree to differ. They have divided us into different denominations and political parties, and placed us on opposing sides in debates passionate enough to prevent effective cooperation in many areas of life. Yet all these opposing views are defended as truly 'biblical'.

In the light of such experience it is hardly surprising that claims to the 'sufficiency' and 'perspicuity' of Scripture have needed to be hedged about with qualifications such as I included in attempting to define the terms above ('at least in principle', 'the intelligent use of principles', 'an unbiased interpreter', 'sufficiently to be able to submit appropriately', 'taken as a whole', etc). While there would still be general agreement that Scripture is sufficient and clear to lead us to salvation, the experience of exegetical and hermeneutical division must surely make us cautious of assuming that on any given matter of either doctrinal or ethical debate an appeal to Scripture can always be expected to yield immediate agreement even among convinced evangelicals. We are increasingly becoming aware that the authority of Scripture is, and must be, mediated to us through the interpretation of Scripture, and that the latter is a human and inexact science.

Changing our minds

Why then, in the light of the long history of evangelical disagreements, has the issue of the ordination of women to the priesthood proved so surprisingly uncomfortable among evangelical Anglicans? Is it perhaps because we have become so used to being paedobaptists or anti-paedobaptists, creationists or evolutionists etc that we no longer notice the disconcerting implications of these divisions for our understanding of how the authority of Scripture works? We have endowed our theological and ecclesiological divisions with the same sort of inevitability that W.S. Gilbert saw in the political realm

> That every boy and every gal
> That's born into the world alive
> Is either a little Liberal
> Or else a little Conservative.

There is some comfort in this sense of group identity. At least we know where we all are.

But what has been disconcerting about the recent debate is that people have been changing sides (in a way which Gilbert never envisaged!). Not too many years ago you would have had to go a long way to find an evangelical Anglican who favoured the ordination of women to the priesthood. Most of us took it as axiomatic that women must not hold positions of authority in the church (though interestingly the ordination of women as *deacons*, with a role which included preaching and teaching in church, seems to have met with little resistance). Saint Paul had made the position quite clear, and that was enough for us. Yet when it came to the crucial vote in the General Synod in 1992, it was apparently the votes of evangelical members which swayed the decision in favour of women priests, and now the majority of evangelicals seem to be found on that side of the fence, no doubt with varying degrees of conviction. What has happened to the earlier evangelical consensus? How can those who hold to the authority of the same unchanging Scripture change their minds?

In the light of Christian experience I would like to suggest that to change one's mind is neither an unprecedented nor a reprehensible thing to do. An analogy which has often been suggested to the present debate about the ordination of women is the discovery by Christians in the early nineteenth century that slavery was not after all an essential feature of the way God has ordained human society. The two issues are not of course parallel in every way (though at some points the similarity is a little too close for comfort), but for our present purpose the point is valid. It would be hard now to find a Christian who would argue that slavery is according to the will of God and is required by a biblical ethic. Yet slavery is there, accepted and uncondemned, in both Old and New Testaments, and it would have been easy for an eighteenth-century Christian to argue that the emancipation of slaves was a product of the secular liberal agenda which it was the duty of all faithful Christians to resist in the name of the biblical world-view. It was only gradually that Christians were led to realise that Scripture speaks with more than one voice on the issue, and that the simple appeal to the cultural pattern which appears on the surface of the biblical text may need to yield to more fundamental ethical principles which, while not explicitly applied to slavery in Scripture, must ultimately lead to its abolition. It can hardly be denied that it was the changing nature and values of secular society which were the catalyst that led Christians to re-examine their understanding of the Bible on this issue, but none of us would now, with hindsight, wish to argue that Christians at that time should not therefore have been willing to allow their traditional understanding to be challenged, and their biblical hermeneutic to develop under the influence of new thinking and new situations in the world around them. So they changed their minds, and none of us now would have had it otherwise.[6]

And even within the pages of Scripture we see examples of the re-evaluation of the bearing of scriptural principles in the light of new situations, leading the people of God to approve what, on scriptural grounds, they would previously have condemned. Even New Testament Christians could change their minds! Probably the most striking example is the so-called Council of Jerusalem in Acts 15, at which the church's leaders concluded, in the light of the experience of the Gentile mission of Paul and Barnabas, that Gentiles could properly be received as full members of the church without first becoming Jews. Obvious as this may seem to us (as Gentile Christians!), for a traditionally-minded Jewish Christian it must have been a profoundly disorientating conclusion, and, more importantly for our purposes, one which apparently flew in the face of the plain teaching of Scripture.

On the basis of the Old Testament concept of the chosen people, first-century Jews kept themselves apart from Gentile uncleanness. Their circumcision and their adherence to the Mosaic laws marked them out as God's special people, and the strict food-laws of Leviticus made it effectively impossible for them to share table-fellowship

---

6 Note especially the recent article by K. Giles in *EQ* 66 (1994) 3-17 entitled (with an intriguing pre-echo of the title of these lectures!) 'The Biblical Argument for Slavery: Can the Bible Mislead? A Case Study in Hermeneutics'. Giles points out how those who favour 'the permanent subordination of women' have felt obliged to argue that the Bible never endorsed slavery – otherwise their case for the permanent validity of the supposed scriptural norm in relation to gender would be undermined by their unwillingness to maintain slavery as well. By demonstrating that the Bible does in fact endorse slavery, he therefore claims to have shown 'that Scripture can endorse social structures no longer acceptable, just as we have learnt that the Bible can endorse scientific ideas no longer tenable' (p.4).

with those outside the covenant. They looked back with pride to the drastic measures taken by Ezra and Nehemiah to eliminate mixed marriages and so to preserve the purity of the people of God (Ezra 9–10; Neh. 13.23–31). Jewish Christians who inherited this national exclusiveness could appeal also to both the example and the teaching of Jesus himself, who restricted his mission (with minor exceptions) to the Jews and imposed the same restriction on his first disciples (Mt. 10.5–6; 15.24). To contemplate the entry of Gentiles on equal terms into the people of God must have seemed a betrayal of this whole national heritage, and, they may well have argued, a clear contravention of the plain teaching of Scripture. The dangerously 'liberal' agenda of Paul and Barnabas stood clearly opposed to the basic biblical concept of the people of God as it had hitherto been understood.

And yet the church, or at least its leaders gathered at Jerusalem, changed its mind. The account given in Acts 15 is too brief to allow us to overhear all the arguments. The most prominent feature of the debate seems to have been the accounts by Paul and Barnabas of their experience of God's blessing on the Gentile mission, together with Peter's reminder of his own experience of 'conversion' from Jewish exclusivism to the Gentile mission as a result of a direct revelation (as recounted in Acts 10–11). But it is significant that the final verdict of the Council, as expressed by James, while it was no doubt strongly influenced by these accounts of the undeniable work of God, also sets the debate in the context of biblical authority, by quoting a scriptural text (Amos 9.11–12) which points forward to a new phase of God's work in which the Gentiles would find their due place. And of course Amos 9.11–12 is by no means alone, but represents a strong stream of 'alternative' theology in the Old Testament which runs from the call of Abraham to be a blessing to all the families of the earth (Gen. 12.3), through the mission of the Isaianic servant to be a light to the nations (Is. 49.6), through to the vision of the world-wide worship of Yahweh in Malachi 1.11. What the church decided at Jerusalem, under the pressure of undeniably God-directed change, was to prefer one strand of Scriptural teaching over another, to accept that the unchanging revelation of God made provision for changing circumstances and for a development in God's dealings with his world which would leave behind the comfortable security of the phase of Jewish exclusivism, firmly rooted as this had also been in Scripture. 'Biblical teaching', it thus appeared, was no longer as simple and self-evident a concept as it might have seemed. There was a hermeneutical task to be done.

One can hear echoes of this debate again and again in the New Testament. Paul was often conscious of his image, among more conservative Jewish Christians, as a dangerous radical, and found it necessary to argue at length from Scripture (notably in Romans 9–11) for the legitimacy of his Gentile mission. There were, the church historians tell us, members of the Jerusalem church who were unpersuaded by this Pauline 'liberalism', and maintained a strictly Jewish Christian community, later known as the Ebionites, which continued for a time in opposition to the mainstream church but which has left no abiding mark in Christian history. No doubt the Ebionites were convinced that they alone had maintained the true biblical faith. But in fact the work of God went forward not through their unchanging tradition but along new lines, equally based on Scripture, in the hands of those whose hermeneutic was sufficiently alert to recognise that faithfulness to biblical revelation need not, indeed cannot, be equated with resistance to change.

Our study of Acts 15 may seem to have taken us a long way from our subject. It was not, of course, intended to suggest any direct comparison between the issues of Gentile membership of the church and of the ordination of women. My point is simply to illustrate that in the ongoing work of God it is sometimes permissible, indeed necessary, for his people to change their minds. What this example illustrates is also that when such a change of mind takes place, it is not necessarily a matter of abandoning the authoritative teaching of the Bible in favour of a secular agenda, but more likely a matter of discovering that there is more in the Bible than we had realised, that those strands of biblical teaching and practice on which we have been accustomed to rely in relation to a given issue may not be the only aspects of biblical revelation which are relevant to it. We may be faced, as the Jerusalem Christians were faced, with the uncomfortable task of deciding which of apparently competing streams of biblical thought should take precedence in the new situation in which we find ourselves.

In such a decision, however carefully we all try to submit ourselves to the guidance of the Holy Spirit, it is possible, and indeed Christian experience suggests that it is likely, that we will not all agree. There will be some for whom the demands of the Christian mission and the changing context to which it must relate itself require that we re-examine our inherited assumptions, and go back to Scripture to see whether we have yet exhausted its relevance. There will be others who maintain that the scriptural principles which have guided us hitherto must continue to do so and thus must have priority over any new insight which others might claim to have derived from the Bible. There will always be, in other words, both progressives and traditionalists, and it is likely, in the light of long Christian experience, that each will find legitimate ammunition in the Bible with which to promote their cause.[7] It is in just such a situation that evangelical Anglicans now find themselves in relation to the ordination of women to the priesthood.

Two hermeneutical approaches

Those who oppose the ordination of women to the priesthood undeniably have tradition on their side, not only the massive tradition of the Roman Catholic and Orthodox churches, but also the general consensus of evangelical Protestants until relatively recent years. While several of the Protestant churches have for a good number of years appointed women to the equivalent of the role of an Anglican priest, even within those churches there has been a more conservative element which has been uneasy over such appointments or has directly opposed it on scriptural grounds.

The hermeneutical basis for this position, at least as

---

7 The division between the 'strong' and the 'weak' to which Paul addresses himself in Romans 14.1 – 15.6 offers a further New Testament example of such disagreement over the hermeneutical implications of Old Testament texts, with reference in this instance to dietary and other aspects of Christian life-style. Paul's response to that division may have a great deal to teach us about the right attitude to adopt in our current debate over the ordination of women. His clear

espoused by evangelicals (for the Roman Catholic and Orthodox it might look rather different!) has been focused on two main contentions.

1. There are a small number of passages in the New Testament which explicitly rule against a vocal or authoritative rule for women in the church. Principal among these has been 1 Timothy 2.8–15, but appeal is also made to 1 Corinthians 14.33b–36 and, in a rather different way, to 1 Corinthians 11.2–16.

2. It would not be fair, however, to depict this viewpoint as based on these passages alone. Together with them must be taken the more general New Testament assertion that there is a priority between men and women which results in a God-given role-distinction involving the exercise of authority by men and the 'submission' of women to this authority. This relationship is often summed up in the metaphor of the man as 'head' of the woman which appears in 1 Corinthians 11.3 and Ephesians 5.23. While it is admitted that the latter passage is concerned with the marriage relationship and not, explicitly at least, with ministry in the church, the former is apparently set in a wider context. In any case, however the specific metaphor of the 'head' may be deployed by Paul, the general principle of authority and submission is one which appears more widely in the New Testament and which is assumed to underlie the specific prohibitions of authority to women in the church context.

It is these scriptural arguments, rather than the tradition of the non-Protestant parts of the church, which carry most weight with evangelicals who oppose the ordination of women to priesthood. For them these New Testament passages enshrine a permanent principle which must apply to all church contexts in all times and places, and which rules out the holding of authoritative office in the church by any women anywhere. That is the way God has made us, and as Christians we are not at liberty to infringe his provision, whatever may happen in society at large.

It will be my purpose in the next chapter to explore the more general contention summed up in the term 'headship', and in the third chapter to look in more specific

---

personal support for the 'strong' position is combined with a respect for the conscience of the 'weak', and a plea to both sides to make due allowance for each other's sincerity rather than indulging in point-scoring.

detail at 1 Timothy 2.8–15 which has become for many the touchstone of the hermeneutical debate on this issue.

On the other side of the debate the hermeneutical considerations are usually more wide-ranging, but again it may be suggested that there are two main areas of contention involved.

1. Just as there are specific passages which forbid the authoritative or teaching role of women in the church, there are others which appear not only to allow but to encourage it. Even 1 Corinthians 11, at the same time as asserting the subordinate role of women, accepts their activity in praying and prophesying in the church (in apparent conflict with the silence required in 1 Corinthians 14.34–35). Most notable is the remarkable sequence of references to women among Paul's co-workers in Romans chapter 16, and the roles which they appear to have played in the Pauline churches. One of them, Priscilla (Prisca, Romans 16.3) meets us elsewhere in the New Testament, and it is an interesting question how her activities there recorded relate to the 'headship' principle. A specific text often quoted in this connection is Paul's assertion that in Christ there is now 'no male and female' (Gal. 3.28). While it is true that this text does not specifically mention ministry in the church, its possible implications for such ministry are no less open to discussion than in the case of the 'subordinationist' passages mentioned above (most of which likewise have no explicit bearing on church ministry). It will be these passages which form the basis of our discussion in the fourth chapter.

2. But again, as for the other viewpoint, it is not fair to suggest that those in favour of the ordination of women base their argument merely on a few texts. In their case there are two wider issues to consider. One is the whole issue of the 'trajectory' of the Bible's attitude to women, through the Old Testament, the ministry of Jesus (especially in the light of the attitudes found in Jewish culture at the time), and into the apostolic church, so that Galatians 3.28 may be perceived not as an isolated 'liberationist' text but as the apex of a growing structure of challenge to the patriarchal assumptions of ancient society. The other is the much more fundamental hermeneutical issue of the changing context of Christian disciple-

ship, raising the question whether what was appropriate and even necessary in New Testament times can simply be assumed to apply equally to our own very different times and culture. To put it simply, even if one concludes that Paul forbade women in Ephesus and Corinth to hold positions of authority in the church, does this mean that they may not do so in our churches today? Indeed, had Paul been writing to twentieth-century Manchester, would he have said the same as he said to first-century Ephesus?

Exegesis and application

In setting out the opposing hermeneutical approaches I have focused initially (and will continue to do so in much of what follows) on the exegesis of specific passages. What did Paul really mean? What really was going on in the Pauline churches? This is the essential basis for any intelligent discussion of the issue by those who seek to be guided by Scripture. We must try, if at all possible, to agree on what the text actually meant and on what really was the situation in the apostolic church, both in terms of their practice and of the ideology which underlay it. But the concluding remarks in the previous section have indicated that when our exegetical work is done to the best of our ability, we may not yet have got to the heart of the issue. It is quite possible to agree on what Paul said and why, but to continue to disagree as to its relevance to our own situation. Exegesis must be followed by application, and the two tasks are not the same.

It is here that we need a great deal of restraint and mutual understanding in the way we conduct our discussion. The easy way at this point is to retreat into slogans. Those who stand on the traditional side can easily assume, and sometimes do, that anyone who questions the direct application of Paul's pronouncements to the modern church scene is simply evading the authority of Scripture. If it is a mark of the true evangelical to submit to 'the plain teaching of the Bible', then all true evangelicals must be opposed to the authoritative ministry of women, because Paul was. For some who take this position, in effect exegesis *is* application: once the text is understood, its application to any and every church context follows automatically. But those on the other side of the debate can, and sometimes do, equally easily dismiss the alternative position as hermeneutically naive, as mindlessly quoting proof-texts without recognising either that the horizon of the biblical writers is different from ours or that even within the pages of the Bible there is development and growth, so that not all biblical texts necessarily carry the same relevance to a later context.

While no doubt these portraits, like most caricatures, may sometimes be not far from the truth, the debate can and should operate at a level of more mutual respect and understanding, even where in the end we have to agree to differ. For there are people on the 'progressive' side who wish to take exegesis seriously and have no desire simply to dismiss any relevant part of Scripture as unimportant for the discussion, and there are those on the 'traditional' side who recognise the difficulty of the hermeneutical questions, and are keen to argue on the ground of more general biblical principles rather than simply from a few selected texts.

The increasing attention to hermeneutical discussion in the last two decades has shown clearly that whereas most of our energy has traditionally been devoted to the exegetical task, to discovering as accurately as possible what the text meant in its original context, that is in fact only the first, and by far the easier, part of the hermeneutical enterprise. There are of course many texts which remain obscure, because we lack the historical or linguistic information to enable us to unravel their meaning. But in principle (and often, given patience and goodwill, in practice too) it should be possible to reach agreement on the relatively objective question of what the writer actually meant and how the original readers might have expected to understand and respond to it. That, as I say, is the easy part!

Whereas the exegesis of a text is concerned with a relatively fixed point in the past – what the author meant and how the original readers are likely to have understood it – its application moves us into an area of uncomfortable flexibility. The question is not now what the text *meant*, but what it *means* to me in my situation and to you in yours as well as to Christians of many different races and ages in many different parts of the world. The only thing these various points of application are likely to have in common is that each of them is far removed from the specific context and situation for which the biblical book was originally written. The answers given to the hermeneutical question, even with regard to the same passage of Scripture, thus clearly have a potential for richly varied results. And yet until such application has been worked out, the hermeneutical task remains only half done, and the practical cash-value for any given reader of studying the Bible still remains to be discovered. The whole exercise is in danger of remaining at the level of an antiquarian exercise, fascinating and historically important no doubt, but of limited relevance to the life and faith of Christians today. The hermeneutical task is inescapable, if the Bible is to be given meaningful authority in the world today, and yet to enter into it is to open up the possibility of far more wide-ranging disagreement than the exegetical question would normally allow. It is to leave behind the comfortable security of the appeal to what is 'obvious', and to recognise that even our most hallowed traditions of interpretation may be open to question.

Lest this be thought an unnecessarily alarmist approach to the interpretation of the Bible, let us look at a few relatively uncontroversial but varied examples.

Many pages of the Old Testament are devoted to detailed prescriptions for the offering of animal sacrifice, yet few Christians today regard these regulations as literally applicable to Christian discipleship. Behind this conventional and largely unthinking assumption lies an important hermeneutical decision about the development through Scripture of God's revelation concerning the means to a right relationship with himself, the climactic role of Jesus as the 'fulfilment of the law', the recognition of spiritual principles within the sacrificial laws which may find appropriate expression in Christian devotion without the literal continuation of sacrifice, etc. It is obviously true in this area that a simple reading-off of contemporary Christian behaviour from the 'plain meaning' of the Levitical laws is not at all self-evident to most Christians today. However little most of us may have thought about it, a sophisticated process of hermeneutical reorientation has taken place.

Or, to take a New Testament example, both Paul in Romans 13.1–7 and Peter in 1 Peter 2.13–17 set out a clear and uncompromising ethic of submission to the (pagan) authorities of both imperial and local government in their day. Most modern Christians do not live under an autocratic pagan imperial régime, and the practical cash-value of the apostolic precepts, clear and unqualified as they are, remains a matter of controversy. A catalogue of the different ways in which Christian interpreters have evaded the 'plain meaning' of these texts would take a long and fascinating chapter of its own, and one which our present focus does not allow us to indulge in; but you do not have to read far before you discover that the problem lies not in understanding what Peter and Paul meant, but in working out in what ways if any it is applicable to Christians in a modern liberal democracy, or under a 'Christian' but unacceptable dictatorship, or in the changing circumstances of the communist and post-communist world.

One final example is closer to our subject, and concerns an issue to which we shall return in the next lecture. There seems little doubt that Paul in 1 Corinthians 11.2–16 intends those involved in public worship to have their heads covered if women but uncovered if men. In some parts of the Christian world today this injunction is strictly and literally observed (and head-coverings are kept ready for the use of any women who come unprepared, just as they are kept in Jewish holy places for the use of visiting men!) but much of Western Christendom seems to have had no difficulty in accepting both mitred bishops and bare-headed women. It is intriguing that in circles where Paul's instructions concerning women's subordinate role in worship are regarded as literally applicable today, the same apostle's instructions regarding their headgear are apparently felt to be culturally dispensable, whereas in some African churches where no woman would dream of appearing in church bare-headed those same women may well take a leading part both in the teaching and the leadership of the congregation.

We shall return to 1 Corinthians 11, but for now enough of examples. I hope these are sufficient to make the point that exegesis alone is only the starting-point of hermeneutics. When we have agreed, if we can, on what the biblical writer meant, we still face the far more demanding and potentially divisive question of what the text means for us and of how, if at all, we should use this particular part of the biblical revelation as the 'supreme authority in all matters of faith and conduct'. One of the factors which is likely to affect our decision is whether we can discern a clear unity of thought and instruction throughout Scripture on the issue under discussion, or whether it would be possible to draw different, even diametrically opposed, conclusions on the subject from different parts of Scripture. If the latter proves to be the case, as it undoubtedly does on the issue of the role of women in the church's worship and ministry, there will be difficult decisions to be made as to which parts of the total biblical revelation should take priority for the decision of this issue, and perhaps whether (as in the case of animal sacrifice) a line of development can be discerned which would enable us to regard one passage as more expressive of the ultimate purpose of God than another. This is an important part of the hermeneutical task.

From the general to the particular

In this chapter, having outlined the issue in terms of current Anglican debate, I have so far talked in general terms rather than entering into the specifics of the discussion. I have tried to indicate why I regard this particular issue as a valuable 'test-case for biblical hermeneutics', and to set out in more general terms the sort of hermeneutical issues which it raises, and which must be addressed if we are to progress towards mutual understanding, if not agreement. Much of what I have said in this first chapter has a wider bearing than merely on the issue of the ordination of women to the priesthood. I have tried to show how fundamental such hermeneutical discussion is to many areas of theological and practical disagreement among Christians. Without it all our talk about the authority of the Bible has very limited cash-value. To claim to live and think under that authority is, whether we like it or not, to be committed to responsible hermeneutics, and it would do a lot for the mutual respect and understanding of Christians if that fact were more widely recognised.

None of what I have said in this chapter is, of course, new or original; it has long been the stuff of theological discussion. But I have tried to set it out in such a way as to persuade those who rather pride themselves on not being theologians, and take their stand on the simple appeal to the 'plain meaning' of Scripture, that it is not quite as easy as that. Molière's M. Jourdain was overjoyed to discover that 'For more than forty years I have been speaking prose without knowing it'.[8] Similarly, all Christians who have read their Bibles and asked 'What has this to say to me?' have been doing hermeneutics, no doubt largely unconsciously and even instinctively, even if they had never heard the word. To recognise what we are doing may open the way to doing it better.

In what follows we shall try to keep these general considerations in mind, but from here on I intend to focus more specifically on the issues raised in connection with the debate over the ordination of women. It is my hope that the discussion will naturally raise the sort of issues discussed in this chapter, and in so doing will prove to be a suitable 'test-case for biblical hermeneutics'.

---

8 Molière, *Le Bourgeois Gentilhomme*, Act II Scene iv.

CHAPTER TWO

Men and Women in the New Testament:

Authority and Submission in the Home – and in the Church?

We have seen in the first chapter that underlying the opposition by some evangelical Anglicans to the ordination of women to the priesthood is the conviction that the New Testament lays down a God-given order of priority in various aspects of human life, most particularly in the home, whereby it is the role of men to exercise authority and of women to submit to that authority. If this is true in other aspects of Christian life, how much more should it be true in the church's worship? If therefore the role of priest involves the exercise of authority over men, it cannot be right for that office to be open to women.

It is with this underlying concept of the roles of men and women, rather than with the specific passages which are thought to bear more directly on the issue, that this chapter is concerned. Of course the two are inseparably connected, insofar as the specific passages are understood to presuppose and to draw their force from this underlying theology of the sexes. But it may prove helpful to look at the broader issue first, before we turn to the more specific exegesis in the next chapter.

Priesthood and authority

Before considering the New Testament data, it is important for our purposes to understand how this issue relates to the specific question of Anglican priesthood.[1] I apologise to those for whom the following section is either already familiar ground or touches on an area of current church life which you feel you neither need nor want to know about. But if I am to fulfil my declared aim of showing how hermeneutical issues have been raised by the current Anglican debate, we cannot avoid a brief analysis of the context within which that debate takes place.

This is not, of course, the place to attempt to set out a full theology of priesthood as it is understood in Anglican circles. That would in any case be a difficult task, since within the range of Anglican theology many different, and sometimes mutually exclusive, understandings of priesthood may be found. Since, however, our concern in this book is with the opposition to the ordination of women to the priesthood as this is found among *evangelical* Anglicans, I need to set out first what it is about the office of priest which those of an evangelical persuasion may feel to be inappropriate for a woman.

Evangelical Anglicans, if they have thought about the issue at all (and not all have!), generally hold a view of priesthood which is, to use a convenient though rather blunt slogan, functional rather than ontological. In other words, what distinguishes a priest on this view is the role which he (or she?!) is authorised to fulfil within the church, rather than the belief that ordination conveys a special 'character' which makes the one ordained different in kind from other Christians.

Most of the tasks undertaken by the Anglican priest can be, and often are, exercised equally by deacons or lay people (and in both these latter categories women are permitted to exercise the same roles as men). These shared tasks include not only administration and pastoral care but also teaching and preaching. Since women were made deacons in 1987 (and indeed before that either as lay people or as deaconesses) they have shared fully in the teaching and preaching roles in most Anglican churches, and this does not seem to have been felt to be a problem

1 See above chapter 1 note 1 for the term 'priest' as used in an Anglican context, and for the reason why I have chosen in this book to use it in preference to the term 'presbyter' by which many evangelical Anglicans prefer to designate the same office.

among most of those evangelical Anglicans who are opposed to their ordination to priesthood. What is it, then, about Anglican priesthood which is different in principle?

To answer that question in terms of specific roles in the church's worship yields a surprisingly limited list. In Anglican worship only a priest may pronounce absolution and blessing and may preside at the celebration of the eucharist. And that is the complete list – other roles may in practice normally fall to the priest, but in appropriate circumstances there is no objection in principle to their being exercised by deacons and/or lay people. Even at the eucharist large parts of the service may be, and often are, delegated to other members of the congregation, but the eucharistic prayer and the breaking of the bread remain the province of the priest alone.

Is it then these functions which some evangelical Anglicans are so anxious to reserve for men only, even though they have no objection to women preaching? Such a position would be hard to defend from an evangelical perspective, and I suspect that most of those evangelicals who oppose the ordination of women to priesthood would have no problem about women fulfilling any one of these functions which in Anglican tradition are reserved for priests. Many evangelicals in the Church of England have a profound dislike of clerical monopoly, and would be only too glad to see such restrictions relaxed.[2] So why are some of those same evangelicals opposed to women being ordained as priests?

This puzzling result was reached by setting up the question in the wrong way. We asked what are the specific roles in worship which are restricted to priests, and on that basis could see no obvious grounds why those evangelicals who permit women to be deacons (and thus to be authorised to preach) should resist their fulfilling also these other functions. But the heart of the issue is

---

2 In July 1994 an unsuccessful attempt was made in the General Synod of the Church of England to gain approval for lay presidency at the eucharist. The move originated from, and was largely supported by, people within the evangelical camp, many of whom are also opponents of the priesthood of women. So we have the intriguing situation that some of those most firmly opposed to women becoming priests and thus being authorised to preside at the eucharist are among those who are strongly in favour of allowing lay people (presumably male?) to fulfil that same role.

elsewhere: it is a matter of authority. A deacon in the Church of England remains a subordinate officer, under the authority of the incumbent[3] responsible for the parish or group of parishes. And it is priests who, as a matter of fact, become incumbents. In other words, the distinctive function of priests is not primarily specific acts in the context of worship, but an overall role of leadership in the parish. It is such leadership which, it is argued, it is not appropriate in the light of New Testament teaching for women to exercise. For a woman deacon to teach and preach, on this view, is acceptable since this role is delegated by and exercised under the authority of a male incumbent. But it is not acceptable for a woman to be 'in charge' of the local congregation.[4]

In theory this argument might be felt to carry less weight today than it would have done a few decades ago. The talk these days is all about the 'collaborative' ministry of the whole people of God and thus about shared leadership. Whereas previously the vicar generally thought of himself, and was expected by his congregation to do so, as 'in charge' of the parish, a 'leader' whom it was the responsibility of the laity to follow and obey, most clergy these days prefer, at least in theory, to think of themselves and to be seen by others as 'enablers', 'encouragers' and 'trainers' of the whole congregation. The modern form of the service of ordination declares that a priest is 'servant and shepherd among the people to whom he is sent', and 'servant-leadership' has become for many the expressed ideal of the priest's role.

But even a 'servant-leader' is still a leader, and whatever the theory the practice is still that the incumbent is the manager of the local branch of the church enterprise.

---

3 The term 'vicar' would probably be more easily recognised by many who are not familiar with the Anglican system, but since for historical reasons some parishes have vicars and some rectors (and nowadays many groups of parishes have a number of vicars under a single 'Team Rector'), 'incumbent' is the only unambiguous term available to describe the clergyman (or now clergywoman) in charge

4 It is of course possible for a person ordained as priest to decline to serve as an incumbent, and to complete his/her ministry as a curate or perhaps as a team vicar under the authority of a team rector. This might in theory be an acceptable route for an evangelical woman who believed that she should remain in a 'subordinate' role. In practice, however, this is an unusual course, and might not be widely understood, so that it is presumably felt wiser to draw the line at the point of ordination as priest.

Clergy speak quite naturally of 'my parish', and the people expect the incumbent to provide firm leadership, however much they may value and exercise their right to voice their opinions in the Parochial Church Council. And this role of leadership which continues to be taken for granted reflects also the incumbent's legal status and responsibility. On appointment to a parish the incumbent is inducted by the archdeacon into 'the real and actual possession of this Church and benefice, with all the rights and responsibilities belonging to it'. The incumbent is, under the bishop, in charge of and responsible for its proper functioning as a part of the Church of England. Whatever the theory about collaborative leadership the incumbent is, in effect, the boss.

This excursion into the inner workings of the Church of England was necessary in order to give more tangible content to the current Anglican discussion with regard to ordination to the priesthood. The question before us, then, is whether in the light of New Testament teaching it is appropriate for a woman to hold that office, and as such to exercise authority over the men as well as the women of the congregation.

The 'submission' of women in the New Testament[5]

The Greek verb ὑποτάσσομαι, usually translated 'submit' or 'be subject', is surprisingly prominent in the New Testament. A more etymological translation might be 'to order oneself under', since the root from which ὑποτάσσομαι is derived (the verb τάσσω and the noun τάξις) is concerned with 'order', and the Greek middle voice regularly carries a reflexive sense. Etymology is not necessarily, of course, a true guide to usage, but in this case the wider use of related terms in the New Testament reveals (mainly, but not only, in the writings of Paul) a wide-ranging concept

---

5 Among the many books offering a 'traditional' account of this issue on the basis of Scripture, the massive advocacy by S.B. Clark, *Man and Woman in Christ* (Ann Arbor: Servant Books, 1980) has been influential; briefer but more trenchant is W. Neuer, *Man and Woman in Christian Perspective* (London: Hodder & Stoughton, 1990). A more 'progressive' account, equally firmly based on Scripture, is offered by, among many others, M. Hayter, *The New Eve in Christ* (London: SPCK, 1987) and by the wide-ranging symposium edited by A. Mickelsen, *Women, Authority and the Bible* (Downers Grove: IVP, 1986).

of an 'order' which God has designed for human society at many levels, and within which it is appropriate that we each find our due role. It is within this overarching concept of 'order' that the injunctions to 'submit' find their place. To submit is to recognise your place within the God-given order of society and to act appropriately to that place, by accepting the authority of those to whom God has entrusted it. It is a principle which is, of course, easier to enunciate than to put into practice, as the long history of Christian struggles with Paul's teaching on submission to civil authorities makes only too clear; but it is a principle which is widely recognised in the New Testament.

This ideal of 'submission' applies not only to women. The verb is used to describe the Christian's proper attitude to political authorities (Rom. 13.1,5; Tit. 3.1; 1 Pet.2.13), and Paul in Romans 13.1–2 brings together an impressive collection of cognate terms to reinforce the idea of a God-given order in society ('be subject' is ὑποτάσσομαι, 'instituted' is τάσσομαι, 'resists' is ἀντιτάσσομαι, and 'appointed' represents the cognate noun διαταγή). Slaves should 'submit' to their masters (Tit. 2.9; 1 Pet. 2.13), children to their parents (1 Tim. 3.4 – even Jesus did, Lk. 2.51!) church members to their church leaders (1 Cor. 16.16; 1 Pet. 5.5) and, more broadly, all of us to one another (Eph. 5.21). Above all, of course, all of us must 'submit' to God (Heb. 12.9; Jas. 4.7), as the church must 'submit' to Christ (Eph. 5.24). All these are uses of the verb ὑποτάσσομαι (or, in 1 Tim. 3.4, its cognate noun ὑποταγή). The same concept of 'order' emerges strikingly in 2 Thessalonians 3.6–12 (cf 1 Thes. 5.14), where the offence generally translated into English as 'idleness' is more literally 'being out of order'; those who refuse to work are failing to pull their weight in the 'order' which God has established in society. The church too in its corporate life and worship is meant to operate on the basis of 'order' (1 Cor. 14.40; Col. 2.5, both using the noun τάξις).[6]

It is against this broader background that we can best understand the idea that in marriage the wife is expected to 'submit' to her husband (Eph. 5.22; Col. 3.18; Tit. 2.5; 1 Pet. 3.1,5). In marriage, as in other aspects of society,

---

6 Note also the centurion's description of himself as 'placed under authority', using the same terminology, ὑπὸ ἐξουσίαν τασσόμενος (Lk. 7.8). A similar 'order' operates in the army!

there is an 'order' which God has appointed, and it is appropriate for the wife's attitude and behaviour towards her husband to reflect this. Not that the husband is free of responsibility either: he too has his complementary role to fulfil, spelled out in terms of 'love', 'consideration' and 'honour' (Eph. 5.25–33; Col. 3.19; 1 Pet. 3.7). Moreover, the whole discussion of the marriage relationship in Ephesians is introduced by the injunction that all disciples should 'be subject to one another out of reverence for Christ' (Eph. 5.21). It is remarkable that Paul conspicuously avoids calling on the wife to 'obey' her husband, even though he uses this verb in the parallel passages relating to children and slaves (Eph. 6.1,5; Col. 3.20,22). It is the Anglican Prayer Book, not the New Testament, which has interpreted the marriage relationship in terms of 'obedience'![7] There is thus a mutuality in the marriage relationship which is different from that of children to parents or slaves to masters. Indeed in 1 Corinthians 7.4 Paul takes this mutuality so far as to declare the wife's 'authority over her husband's body' no less than his over hers.

In the home – or in the church as well?

But, even with this proviso, the apostolic teaching is clearly that within the marriage relationship the husband should exercise authority and the wife 'be subject' to it, because that is the way God has designed the relationship of the sexes.

If this is the situation within marriage, does it follow that a similar 'order' should be observed in society in general, and in the affairs of the church in particular? Are Christians who aim to be guided by Scripture thus obliged to oppose not only the ordination of women to the priesthood, but also any role for women in society which gives them authority over men? In contemporary Britain this would rule out the Queen, the Speaker of the House of Commons, the Director of Public Prosecutions, the

---

7 Even the *Alternative Service Book* (1980) retains the verb 'obey' in an optional alternative form of the marriage vows! The nearest approach in the New Testament to such an injunction is 1 Peter 3.6 where Sarah is commended as a model for Christian wives: her 'submission' was demonstrated in that she 'obeyed Abraham and called him lord'.

head of MI5 and several other prominent figures in society, not to mention large numbers of head-teachers, senior police officers and the like. Does the Christian duty of submission to the governing authorities cease to apply when the Prime Minister is a woman (as some may well have wished not too long ago!)?

To raise such questions is, of course, to realise that, whatever some may wish to be the case, the reality of life in modern Britain is such that it is impossible to apply a general principle of male authority to society at large, and most Christians seem to have been able to settle without too much discomfort into that reality. But in any case it seems likely that in reaching this position they have the New Testament on their side, since its injunctions for women to submit to men are not applied to the structures of society in general, but to the marriage relationship. First-century society was of course strongly male-dominated, and that environment is reflected in various ways in the relationship between the sexes which we can discern in the New Testament, but the New Testament writers nowhere state that this fact of society is either inevitable or part of the divine purpose. Rather it remains, like the institution of slavery, a part of the given scene which is neither commended nor directly disputed, but which will in due course be undermined as Christian people are enabled to apply the wider principles of New Testament ethics in the context of a changing world-order.

To reach this conclusion may seem to have cut the ground away also from under those who oppose the ordination of women to the priesthood on the basis that the New Testament upholds a general principle of male authority. But there are at least two reasons why we might hesitate in drawing this conclusion.

1. What God intends for society and what he intends for the church are not necessarily the same. The New Testament in many ways indicates that it is the calling of the church, as the people of God, not to imitate the norms and values of secular society. Rather, its structures should reflect the God-given ideal of human relationships which society as a whole too often ignores. The church should thus, by its very nature, constitute a challenge to the norms accepted by society at large. Its essence is in being different.

Should we then argue that it is the calling of the church to uphold a principle of male authority which society as a whole has increasingly abandoned (though many would say that even in secular society the process has still not gone far enough!)? Should the church, by ordering its affairs firmly along the lines of male leadership and female submission hold up to the world an image of the better way? Yet there is, as we have seen above, no indication in the New Testament that such a way *is* better for society at large. Male leadership may be a reality in the first-century world, but it is not presented to us an an ideal for human life in general, other than in the marriage relationship, and it is at least a valid question whether it is acceptable to extrapolate from marriage to the wider structures of society.

If there is doubt about whether male domination is right for society at large, however, perhaps there is one rule for the world and another for the church? Does God then intend his people to operate along lines which he has not laid down for the rest of humanity? This is in principle a plausible scenario, but to accept it as the biblical pattern we would surely need some indication in Scripture that the church, and not just the family, is intended to operate under male leadership. And that brings us to the second reason for caution in assuming that because the principle of male leadership is explicitly presented in the context of marriage it has nothing to say about church structures.

2. Our survey of New Testament uses of ὑποτάσσομαι and its cognates above was in fact not complete. While the majority of injunctions to women to 'submit' to men refer to the context of the home, there are two passages where similar language is used with reference to the church. In 1 Corinthians 14.34–35, while discussing what should and should not happen when the church comes together for worship, Paul instructs women not to speak in church, but rather to be silent, to be 'subordinate', as the law says, and to refer any questions to their own husbands at home. In this case, the close juxtaposition of the idea of subordination with that of asking their husbands strongly suggests that it is again the marriage relationship which is in focus, that these are married women who when in church should leave their husbands to be the spokesmen for the partnership. We shall return to this passage later, and

shall notice then how puzzling and obscure commentators have found this instruction to be.

But the other passage lends itself less easily to being subsumed under the discussion of the marriage relationship. This is, of course, 1 Timothy 2.8–15, where the prohibition on a woman teaching or having authority over a man is preceded by the injunction that she should 'learn in silence with full submission (ὑποταγή)'. We shall devote most of the next chapter to an attempt to unravel the significance of this passage for our subject, and I do not wish here to anticipate that discussion. It is possible that the 'man' over whom she is not to usurp authority does not refer to the men of the church in general but rather specifically to her husband (which would make the following allusion to the respective roles of Adam and Eve and to childbirth the more appropriate). But even if this were the case, the injunction to learn in silence and not to teach appears, especially in the context of vv. 8–10, to have a wider application to the woman's role in the church, not merely to her relationship with her husband. For the time being, therefore, and in anticipation of a fuller discussion of this passage in the next chapter, we may conclude that a reasonable case can be made on the basis of this passage that the language concerning women's 'submission', while primarily applied to the marriage relationship, can also have a wider relevance to what happens in church.

'The husband is the head of the wife'

I have so far in this chapter avoided using a term which has become a frequent slogan in this aspect of the debate, 'headship'. The word is heard so often in discussions of the respective roles of men and women today that some people may be surprised to learn, firstly, that there is no Greek noun in the New Testament which corresponds to the English abstract noun 'headship', secondly, that the metaphor of the man as 'head' occurs only twice in the New Testament (1 Cor. 11.3; Eph. 5.23), and, thirdly, that in at least one of those uses there is no reason in context to think that the metaphor has any relevance to the issue of women's ministry in the church: it is, in Ephesians 5.23, simply a way of expressing the marriage relationship. I have therefore thought it wise hitherto to find other ways of expressing what is meant these days by 'headship', and would like now to look at the two uses of the metaphor of the man as 'head' to see how they may relate to the issue under discussion. This will then lead into a fuller examination of the meaning and implications of 1 Corinthians 11.2–16, the one passage within which the term 'head' is used and which does have a bearing in some sense on what happens in church.

It may seem ridiculous to begin the discussion of κεφαλή, 'head', by pointing out that the word means that part of the body in which the brain, eyes etc are located, and that it is in this literal sense that the term is used in the large majority of its occurrences in the New Testament. But in this case there is value in stating the obvious. I have heard discussions in which protagonists of the different sides in our debate have argued with equal conviction that κεφαλή *means* the one in a position of authority or that κεφαλή *means* 'source'. But of course the word in itself *means* neither of these things. These are differing interpretations of the possible intention of using 'head' as a metaphor, and other possible metaphorical uses could be added, but none of them in itself is *the meaning* of either the Greek κεφαλή or the English 'head'. When the word occurs in other than its literal sense, it is necessary to work out from the context in which it occurs, as part of the writer's argument, as well as from other known metaphorical uses with which we may expect him to have been familiar, why he may have selected this particular metaphor in this context. When we note that Paul uses this same metaphor three times in 1 Corinthians 11.3 to express the very different relationships between Christ and every man, between man and woman, and between God and Christ, it is surely *prima facie* most unlikely that we shall find a simple and unvarying metaphorical sense for 'head'.

Since the head is the part of the body which controls and coordinates the actions of the rest and which is at the top of the body, it is natural, at least for modern readers,[8]

---

[8] S. Bedale, in an article to be considered shortly (*JTS* 5 [1954] 212), says that in the ancient world, despite the advanced views of Hippocrates and Plato, it was generally believed, following Aristotle, that reason and purpose were located in the heart rather than the head, so that the idea of the head as the controlling part

to expect some sense of control or coordination or of superior importance to be found in most metaphorical uses of the term, and this is in fact the case. The few metaphorical uses of κεφαλή in the New Testament illustrate the point. The stone described as 'head of the corner' is presumably the most important stone in the building (Mt. 21.42; Mk. 12.10; Lk. 20.17; Acts 4.11; 1 Pet. 2.7, all quoting LXX Ps. 118.22). When Christ is described as 'head of all rule and authority' (Col. 2.10) he is marked out as the supreme authority to which all others are subject. The only other metaphorical uses of κεφαλή in the New Testament (other than the two which are our concern here) depict Christ as 'head of the church, which is his body' (Eph. 1.22; Col. 1.18; cf. Eph. 4.15; 5.23; Col. 2.19), and the way in which the metaphor is worked out in surrounding verses suggests that Paul intends it to denote the controlling and coordinating function of Christ in relation to his church, whereby it is able to fulfil his purpose and achieve its full potential through its inseparable relation with him on whom it depends for its very existence.

In Ephesians 5.23ff this relationship is worked out in terms of Christ's loving and sacrificial purpose of perfection for his church, taken as a model for the husband's love of his wife (of whom he also is the 'head'). Here we are going well beyond any necessary implications of the metaphor 'head' in itself, but the essential imagery of a controlling and coordinating function seems clearly present.

One of the two uses of 'head' as a metaphor for a man's relation to a woman is in this latter passage (Eph. 5.23). The verb ὑποτάσσομαι occurs in Ephesians 5.21,24 as the correlative to the metaphor of 'head' – as the church 'submits' to its 'head', Christ, so the woman should 'submit' to her 'head', her husband. Here then is a metaphor which picks up the whole 'subordination' theme

of the body would have been 'unintelligible to St. Paul or his readers'. Even if this assertion is true, however (it is strongly disputed, with examples, by W. Grudem, *Trinity Journal* 6 [1985] 42), it does not seem to affect the metaphorical use of 'head' for that which is 'on top', in terms of authority and importance. See further J.A. Fitzmyer, *NTS* 35 (1989) 503–511, who argues from the usage of κεφαλή in the LXX and in Philo that 'a Hellenistic Jewish writer such as Paul of Tarsus could well have intended that κεφαλή in 1 Cor 11.3 be understood as "head" in the sense of authority or supremacy over someone else'.

which we have considered above, and sums it up in the suitably vivid image of the head and the body. The term coheres with what we have already seen to be an important New Testament theme with regard to the relation of husband and wife, but does not take us beyond it for our present purposes, since no implications for the woman's participation in the activities of the church are drawn from it in this passage. It is simply an image for the marriage relationship.

1 Corinthians 11.2–16

The other metaphorical use of κεφαλή with reference to man and woman is however rather different. In 1 Corinthians Paul does not use the imagery found in Ephesians and Colossians of Christ as head of the church (indeed when the body analogy is developed in 1 Corinthians 12 the head appears in v. 21 along with the eye, hand, feet etc as just one of the mutually dependent parts of the body). But in 1 Corinthians 11.2–16,[9] where the issue is whether or not the (literal) head of a woman should be covered in worship, Paul rather whimsically links this literal meaning with a set of metaphorical uses (1 Cor. 11.3) whereby Christ is the 'head' of every man, the man is the 'head' of the woman (or 'wife' – the Greek γυνή can mean either) and God is the 'head' of Christ. Clearly there are important differences between these three relationships, but Paul finds it appropriate to use the term 'head' metaphorically for all of them. This metaphorical use of the term is perhaps maintained in the references to 'dishonouring the head' in vv. 4 and 5 (where there is probably a deliberate ambiguity: the dishonour is inflicted both on the literal head and on Christ as 'head' of the man, or on the man as 'head' of the woman).[10] Thereafter, the term is used in the rest of the passage in its normal literal

9 This passage has been massively discussed both in commentaries and in studies with special reference to the man/woman issue. For a useful guide to some earlier discussion see C. Brown in *NIDNTT* 2 (1976) 159–162. The fullest and one of the most recent commentary discussions is by G.D. Fee, *The First Epistle to the Corinthians* (NICNT. Grand Rapids: Eerdmans, 1987) 491–530; Fee's notes form a valuable bibliography of recent discussion of the subject.

10 So M.D. Hooker, *NTS* 10 (1963/4) 410–411 and several commentators.

sense, to denote that part of the body which should or should not be covered.[11]

But if the metaphorical use of 'head' disappears after v. 5 (if not earlier) other imagery is introduced to fill out Paul's concept of the relationship between man and woman (or husband and wife; the ambiguity of the terms ἀνήρ and γυνή remains throughout). The man is the 'image and glory' of God, while the woman is the 'glory' of the man;[12] the woman is 'out of the man' (ἐξ ἀνδρός), not the man 'out of' the woman, since the man was not created 'because of' the woman, but the woman 'because of the man' (διὰ τὸν ἄνδρα). These different expressions, largely based on reflection on the stories of creation in Genesis 1 and 2, where woman was created literally 'out of' man and in order to be his helper, all have the effect of reinforcing the sense of the priority of the man. Indeed, Paul seems to feel that he may have overstated his case, for he then enters a qualification in vv. 11–12 'Nevertheless, in the Lord woman is not independent of (literally "without") man or man independent of woman. For just as woman came from man, so man comes through woman.' There is, then, not so much a one-way relation of dependence, but rather a mutuality, and this mutual dependence is then grounded in the more fundamental observation that 'all things come from God'.

In the light of this further development of Paul's thought, what may we say about the implications of his choice of the metaphor of 'head' in v. 3? It picks up and plays on the literal term which is the subject of the passage, allowing the teasing ambiguity of vv. 4–5. But that does not mean that it is not seriously intended as a metaphor in itself, as it is in Ephesians 5.23 where no literal use of κεφαλή in the context suggested it. It is clearly a way of expressing priority in some sense, and that sense is such that it can also denote the 'priority' between God

---

11 Since our concern is with the role of women in worship and ministry, and especially the respective roles of men and women, I shall concentrate on the bearing of our passage on this issue rather than on the head-covering issue as such, with all the fascinating cultural questions which it raises, and on which opinions continue to differ widely.

12 Here again, as with the varying uses of the 'head' metaphor in v. 3, the use of the same term 'glory' cannot be pressed to the point of supposing that the relationship between woman and man is of exactly the same kind as that between man and God.

and Christ as well as between Christ and the man, different as each of these relationships is in fundamental ways. Perhaps at the root of this idea is that of *temporal priority*, which is certainly involved in Paul's comments in vv. 8–9 on the priority of the man to the woman in creation. In a rather different sense God 'precedes' Christ, and, in a different sense again, Christ 'precedes' the man. And in each of these varied relationships, the one who is temporally prior is also in some sense the point of origin of the one who follows.[13]

A much-quoted article by S. Bedale in 1954 argued that this idea of temporal priority is fundamental to ancient metaphorical uses of the term 'head', and that therefore in this passage, 'while κεφαλή . . . unquestionably carries with it the idea of "authority", such authority in social relationships derives from a relative priority (causal rather than merely temporal) in the order of being.'[14] Bedale's article has been the basis of a strong move in recent scholarship to suggest that the 'head' metaphor should be understood in terms of 'source' rather than of 'authority',[15] but it is interesting to note that Bedale himself does not regard his argument as weakening the sense of 'authority' in the metaphor, but only as providing a grounding for that authority in the concept of 'priority in the order of being'.[16]

---

13 C.C. Kroeger, in the article mentioned in note 16 below, pp 268–269, 276–277, interestingly quotes from commentaries of Athanasius, Cyril of Alexandria, Basil and Eusebius which all explicitly interpret the κεφαλή of this passage as meaning ἀρχή, 'beginning, origin, source'.

14 S. Bedale, 'The Meaning of κεφαλή in the Pauline Epistles', *JTS* 5 (1954) 211–215.

15 Fee's commentary represents one of the most single-minded presentations of this view.

16 The assertion that '"head" means "source"' has been repeated frequently, with Bedale often quoted as the basic authority for it. This situation provoked W. Grudem (*Trinity Journal* 6 [1985] 38–59) not only to subject Bedale's argument to a critical examination (with special reference to its lack of non-biblical examples) but also to take an independent look at 2,336 instances of the occurrence of κεφαλή in Greek literature (selected from among more than 12,000), to see whether such a sense could be established. Of the (only) 302 metaphorical uses in Grudem's list, he concluded that while 16% referred to a person of superior authority or rank, not a single instance clearly referred to a 'source, origin' (as in 'head of a river'). It should be noted, however, a further 23% of the metaphorical uses are placed in a category which he labels 'Extremity, end, top, starting-point', and it may be felt that the dividing line between the meanings of 'starting-point' and 'source' is rather thin. For a strongly critical analysis of Grudem's article see Fee, *1 Corinthians* 502–503, notes 42–46. In extraordinary contrast to Grudem's article is one by C.C. Kroeger, 'The Classical Concept of

While the 'head' metaphor may carry additional conno-
tations, therefore, among which those of temporal priority
and/or origin are likely to figure, there seems no reason to
see it as significantly different in function from the
language of 'order' and 'submission' which we have noted
above. In Ephesians 5.23 it is used in close connection
with, and as the basis for, such language, and here in 1
Corinthians 11, while the language of 'submission' does
not occur, the sense of priority is equally strongly brought
out in other ways. In each passage, however, it is
important to note that mutual dependence is also stressed
(1 Cor. 11.11–12; Eph. 5.21).

When the metaphor was used in Ephesians 5.23, the
focus was explicitly on the marriage relationship. Here in 1
Corinthians 11 that is not obviously the case. We have
noted above, however, that the terms ἀνήρ and γυνή
which are traditionally here translated 'man' and 'woman'
are also the regular terms for 'husband' and 'wife', so that
it might be suggested that Paul's argument here relates not
so much to man and woman as such, but specifically (and
only?) to man as husband of his wife, and to woman as
wife of her husband. This would mean that Paul is
deliberately extrapolating here from the way the married
relationship works itself out in the home to the way it
affects the respective behaviour of husband and wife
when they are together involved in public worship. In
public no less than in private the wife is to recognise him
as her 'head' and so to express her 'submission' by
keeping a covering on her head which is his 'glory'.

It must be recognised, however, that Paul does not
clearly indicate in this passage that he has in mind only
married people, still less only married couples worship-
ping together. The previous paragraph represents a
possible but not a necessary understanding of the terms
ἀνήρ and γυνή in this context. It is equally possible, and is

---

Head as "Source" ', in G.G. Hull, *Equal to Serve* (Old Tappan, NJ: Revell, 1987)
267–283, which, without specific reference to Grudem but clearly in response to
such arguments as his, offers an impressive array of non-biblical uses of κεφαλή
which in one way or another illustrate its use to mean 'source'. Grudem has
responded at length to these and other criticisms of his article in J. Piper and W.
Grudem (ed), *Recovering Biblical Manhood and Womanhood* (Wheaton: Crossway,
1991) 425–468. This, as they say, could run and run!

indeed more generally believed, that he is thinking of man and woman generically, and applies the metaphor of 'head' to man as man, not just to man as husband.

But even if this latter view is correct, how, if at all, is Paul's argument here relevant to the question of women's ministry in the church? The specific issue under discussion is that of head-covering, a matter of dress, not of ministry. That it is in the context of the Christian assembly that the issue has been raised is hardly surprising, since Paul is writing to the assembled Christians of Corinth. But the 'head' metaphor is used, if not specifically of the marriage relationship, at least only of the general way in which men and women relate to one another, not with regard to the roles they may undertake in a church context. It may be that the principle enshrined in the metaphor may appropriately be extrapolated from the marriage context (and, in this passage, perhaps from a more general understanding of the respective roles of men and women) to a definition of roles in church ministry, but Paul does not here do so.

In that case, neither of the two uses of κεφαλή to describe a man's relation to a woman is in the context of distinguishing their roles in the ministry and leadership of the church. To apply the metaphor in that area must be a matter of consciously extrapolating from Paul's stated application of the metaphor in order to apply it to another subject which, when he does deal with it, Paul himself discusses in different terms. This is not to declare the language of the 'head' necessarily irrelevant to our discussion, but to recognise that in so using it we are going beyond Paul's usage.

I have devoted more time to the two New Testament references to the man as head of the woman than I think they warrant in this connection. I needed to do this because the idea of 'headship' is so often invoked in current debate as if it had a self-evident bearing on the role of women in the ministry of the church. I hope that this discussion, still too brief, has given some reason for believing that its importance has been exaggerated, or at least that its application to the question of the ordination of women, rather than to the marriage relationship, is by no means so obvious as is often assumed.

Women prophets at Corinth

Before leaving 1 Corinthians 11.2–16, however, we may note another feature of the passage which bears more directly on our question. Coincidentally to his main argument Paul indicates that women in the Corinthian congregation were in the habit of 'praying and prophesying' (v. 5), and offers no criticism of this activity. While 'praying' could perhaps be understood of silent, private prayer (though this would reflect more the habits of modern Western Christianity than the likely character of worship in Corinth!), 'prophesying', as Paul goes on to describe it in chapter 14, is a vocal and public activity. It is, moreover, an authoritative activity, as it apparently involves utterances (originating with the Spirit of God rather than from human reasoning) to which the church as a whole is expected to give due attention. Prophecy, in chapter 14, is the most useful and edifying spiritual gift exercised in the church's meeting, and one by which God is understood to communicate with his people through a chosen human medium. 1 Corinthians 11.5 makes it clear that women as well as men might be that medium, and this indicates that their words would carry real authority.

This is in striking contrast to the two passages where 'submission' language is used in relation to the role of women in worship and ministry, one of which (1 Cor. 14.34–35) forbids speech (λαλέω) and requires silence (σιγάω), while the other (1 Tim. 2.11–12) forbids teaching (διδάσκω) and exercising authority (αὐθεντέω), and requires quietness (ἡσυχία). We shall need to keep this tension in mind when we look at those passages more fully in the next chapter, but at least we must conclude from 1 Corinthians 11 that, unless Paul is to be declared inconsistent (or his authorship of any one or more of the three passages to be questioned), these manifestations of submission in Corinth and Ephesus must be in some way consistent with women in Corinth exercising the vocal and authoritative gift of prophecy in the congregation with the apostle's approval. In the final chapter we shall note sufficient other manifestations of women's ministry in the New Testament churches to suggest that, whatever Paul's intention in restricting women's activity in the above passages, 1 Corinthians 11.5 better represents what was actually happening and approved in the churches with which Paul himself was associated.

Authority and submission – conclusions

This chapter has ranged widely. My aim was to explore how far the New Testament supports the notion that (1) God intends men to have authority over women and not *vice versa*, and (2) this principle applies specifically to ministry in the church. My conclusions, briefly, on those two points are as follows:

1. There is in New Testament thinking a concept of 'order' within which man has priority over woman, and it is the role of the latter to 'submit' to (though not necessarily 'obey'?) the former; this concept is, however, linked in Paul's letters with a call for mutual responsibility and indeed mutual submission. This principle of 'subordination' within mutual responsibility is clearly and consistently applied to the marriage relationship in the letters of Paul and Peter. It is much more questionable whether it may also be applied to social and political life in general. Certainly the New Testament does not do so as a matter of principle, even though it inevitably reflects the male-dominated structure of society at the time.

2. The only passages in the New Testament which use the language of 'submission' in relation to women's role in worship or ministry are 1 Corinthians 14.34–35 and 1 Timothy 2.11–12. In the former case the reference to 'their own husbands' makes it likely that the issue is how married couples should behave in church rather than the activity of women in general. In the latter there is at least a case to be made that the principle is applied beyond the marriage relationship. It will be with these two passages, particularly the latter, that we shall be concerned in the next chapter.

We have also been drawn into a discussion of the meaning of Paul's two references to the man as 'head' of the woman. These seem to presuppose the same principle of priority within marriage which is expressed elsewhere in terms of 'submission'. One of them, Ephesians 5.23, is applied directly to the marriage relationship. The other, 1 Corinthians 11.3, *may* have the same reference (though now in relation to their behaviour in church rather than in the home), but may equally be extrapolating from the marriage relationship to a more general view of man, as the first to be created, taking priority over woman. In each passage the 'head' language is appropriately linked with an explicit statement of the mutual dependence of man and woman.

In studying 1 Corinthians 11.2–16 we came, however, to two conclusions significant for our study. (1) Paul is not here addressing the issue of ministry or leadership in the church, but simply how women should dress. To use its language of 'headship' in relation to the former subject, when Paul does not in fact do so here or elsewhere, is at least questionable. (2) It reveals incidentally in v. 5 that women at Corinth did in fact exercise the authoritative ministry of prophecy, and that Paul apparently approved of this. It thus poses a sharp question in relation to the understanding of the two passages which expect women to be silent and submissive in the church context.

1 Corinthians 11.2–16, though often referred to in this connection, seems therefore to offer unpromising material for those who believe that women should not exercise an authoritative ministry in the church today. As a whole it does not relate to the issue at all, and in the one incidental detail where it does, the impression it gives points strongly in the opposite direction. It is interesting moreover to observe that some of those who argue from the 'headship' language of this passage that women should not be ordained do not seem to feel it necessary to enforce the ruling which Paul in fact wrote the passage to lay down, that women should cover their heads in worship. Clearly the hermeneutical process can lead in different directions!

A hermeneutical postscript

I pointed out in the first chapter that the interpretation of the Bible involves two equally important tasks, exegesis and application. This lecture has been almost entirely concerned with exegesis. My aim has been to understand what the New Testament writers do, and do not, say on the subject of the relationship between men and women, and to trace as far as possible the ways in which they themselves work out those ideas and apply them to their own first-century situation. I have so far avoided asking what Paul and the others 'might have said' about our own very different church situation, and what sort of instruction they might have given to us in the context of today's world. But if our study of Scripture is to be of practical value in guiding us to the will of God for his church today, we cannot remain at the exegetical level alone. Difficult as it will be, we must ask whether the principles of Scripture apply in the same way now as they did then, and must be prepared to give reasons for our answers, whether they be positive or negative. Do the same principles apply to our egalitarian culture as applied in the male-dominated world of first-century Corinth or Ephesus? And if they do, do they apply in the same practical ways, or are there now more appropriate ways for the same values to be expressed?

One important part of this hermeneutical process is to try to set any given passage or theme of Scripture within the broader context of Scripture as a whole. Our discussion in this chapter has been limited to only one or two strands and selected passages of the New Testament which are commonly appealed to in this connection. But there is more to the New Testament witness on the subject than these few passages, and not all clearly point in the same direction. To take the most glaring example, it is hard to understand how some of the 'subordinationist' material we have been looking at in this chapter could have been written by the same Paul who wrote that in Christ there is no longer male and female, setting that declaration alongside the parallel assertion that there is no longer slave or free (Gal. 3.28).[17]

It will be the aim of my final chapter to take up this question, to offer a wider view of relevant biblical material, to ask how the various scriptural strands may be fitted together, and to suggest how on that basis a responsible evangelical hermeneutic might respond to the

---

17 One way of attempting to resolve this particular problem has been to suggest that Paul's earlier (and perhaps incautious?) teaching on equality as expressed in Gal. 3.28 was seized on by some 'liberated' women who pressed it to the point of refusing to recognise any gender distinction, with the result that Paul was obliged in later writings to redress the balance!

counter-currents of opinion on the ordination of women to the Anglican priesthood.

But before we can take that broader view, it will be necessary to focus down in more detail on the two passages which have already come to light in this chapter as the primary source for the belief that the New Testament forbids us to ordain women to the priesthood, 1 Corinthians 14.34–35 and 1 Timothy 2.8–15. The discussion will, in the next chapter, remain primarily at the exegetical level – just what was going on at Corinth and Ephesus, why did Paul feel it necessary to take this strongly negative line, and did he intend in these passages to prohibit women taking a vocal and/or authoritative role in the life of the church at all times and in any circumstances? Only after we have tackled these exegetical questions will we be in a position to ask what bearing these passages have on today's world, and how they relate to the other scriptural material which we have to study.

CHAPTER THREE

'I Permit No Woman to Teach or to Have Authority Over a Man':

New Testament Prohibitions and the Ministry of Women Today

In the last chapter we noted that there are two passages in the New Testament which speak of women's 'submission' in the context of church worship and ministry, 1 Corinthians 14.34–35 and 1 Timothy 2.8–15. It is not surprising that it is these two passages (together with 1 Cor. 11.2–16, which we have already considered) which have been at the centre of discussion over the ordination of women to the priesthood. These two passages form the subject of this third chapter, though by far the majority of the space will be devoted to the passage from 1 Timothy, which raises the issue more clearly and specifically. 1 Corinthians 14.34–35 has in fact been given much less weight in current discussion, since everyone, from whatever point of view, seems to find it a hard text to interpret.

Did Paul write these words?

Before we consider the exegesis of these two passages, a word must be said about their authorship. Throughout this book so far I have spoken, as most evangelicals would, of all the letters in the Pauline Corpus as written by Paul. But I am sure I do not need to remind you that a large body of scholarly opinion would hesitate to attribute to Paul not only the Pastoral Epistles, but also other letters, notably Ephesians and Colossians. There is a strong tendency to regard the so-called *Hauptbriefe*

(Romans, 1 and 2 Corinthians and Galatians) as representing the 'real Paul', and to relegate most of the rest of the
corpus to a secondary status, with serious doubts as to the
authorship of at least some letters. For many scholars,
therefore, 1 Timothy, interesting as it may be as a
historical document, can safely (and often with relief!) be
relegated to the side-lines as not representing true
apostolic Christianity, but rather an idiosyncratic position
out of touch with the mainstream development of the
church.

For the evangelical, however, this is not an option.
While evangelicals can and do differ over the question of
the authorship of 1 Timothy, their theology does not allow
them to dismiss it from consideration. Even if Paul did not
write it (and I think he probably did), it remains a part of
the authoritative canon of the New Testament, and cannot
be disregarded in the search for a truly biblical position. Its
authorship therefore does not affect our discussion.

For 1 Corinthians there is no such debate. This letter is,
as all would agree, vintage Paul. But it is worth noting that
however confident they may be about the authorship of
the letter as a whole, a good number of scholars have
questioned whether 14.34–35 is part of the original letter.
We have no textual evidence that the letter ever existed
without these verses, but in several important Greek and
Latin manuscripts of the Western tradition they occur after
14.40, and such variations in placing are sometimes an
indication of a later insertion in the text. On the basis of
this observation several scholars have gone on to notice
how much more easily the argument of the latter part of
the chapter would flow without these two verses, and the
clear conflict between the silence enjoined in these verses
and the praying and prophesying which is allowed in 11.5
has then clinched the argument that these two verses
could not have been part of Paul's original letter. When
even so cautious and experienced a textual critic as
Gordon Fee[1] reaches this conclusion, it must be taken
seriously.

If we were to conclude that the verses are not by Paul,

---

1 G.D. Fee, *1 Corinthians* 699–705; other well-known commentators who incline
to regard the verses as inauthentic include C.K. Barrett and H. Conzelmann. Cf.
J. Murphy-O'Connor, *CBQ* 48 (1986) 90–92.

what would be their status with regard to scriptural authority? Fee assumes that in that case they are 'certainly not binding for Christians'.[2] But they have been part of the canonical text for as far back as we can trace. The same issue would then be raised as in the case of the other major additions to the New Testament text which are found in our Bible, notably Mark 16.9–20 and John 7.53–8.11, though it must be admitted that the textual case against each of those passages is far stronger than in this case. For our present purpose, while bearing in mind their textual uncertainty, it seems appropriate to treat the verses cautiously as part of the canonical New Testament evidence; it will in any case be found that they add little to what may be derived from the unquestionably authentic passage in 1 Timothy 2.

1 Corinthians 14.34–35

These verses occur in the course of Paul's instructions for the better ordering of public worship in Corinth. While not wishing to stifle the gifts of the Spirit, he opposes the uncontrolled and self-centred indulgence in supernatural phenomena which seems to have become the norm in that over-enthusiastic church. His principal criteria are that what is done should be generally edifying (vv. 3–5,12, 17,26) and should exhibit decency and order (v. 40) rather than confusion (v. 33). No distinction between men and women has been made in the instructions for worship in chapter 14 up to verse 33, and 11.5 must lead us to assume that both were equally involved in the activities described. Yet in vv. 34–35, before concluding his discussion of prophecy and other 'spiritual' activity, he unexpectedly calls on women to be silent, and declares it disgraceful for a woman to speak (λαλέω) in church. On any understanding of the context this is a puzzling move, not only because it apparently declares to be self-evidently wrong an activity which Paul has already recognised to be taking place without any expression of disapproval (11.5), but also because it intrudes awkwardly into a discussion of

---

2 *Ibid* 708.

spiritual gifts in worship without any clear indication of how it might fit into that train of thought.

It is no wonder, then, that the authenticity of the passage has been doubted, as we noted earlier; the fact that these two verses are placed at the end of the chapter in many Western manuscripts highlights the problem of their present position. If they are retained here, how may they be explained? We may note the following suggestions.

1. While λαλέω is a very general term for speaking, which is used frequently in 1 Corinthians 14 for the utterance of both prophets and tongue-speakers, is it possible that Paul has in mind here not just any form of speech, but a particular type (such as speaking in a tongue,[3] or giving interpretation of a tongue, or the 'weighing' of a prophecy [v. 29]?) which he regards as inappropriate for women? Unfortunately, there is no indication in these verses of any such specific focus, nor does the rest of the chapter suggest any gender-distinction with relation to the various types of utterance discussed. Moreover, the specific type of speaking which has been under discussion in the immediately preceding verses is prophecy, the one type which he has explicitly recognised as exercised by women in 11.5. In any case, v. 35 suggests that the problem lay in asking questions rather than in making pronouncements.

2. Or might he be using λαλέω here in a sense which it carried in classical Greek, but which is not attested elsewhere in the New Testament, to refer not to formal speech but to 'chatter'? Were some women then in the habit of disturbing the worship of the congregation by gossiping loudly or by asking unnecessary questions? Perhaps, but this is conjecture, and it must be admitted that if this was what Paul intended he would have done much better to use a more specific verb, especially since λαλέω has been used throughout this chapter in its normal New Testament sense.

3. Should we then focus our attention on the point noted in the last chapter, that the reference to 'submission'

---

3 This possibility is virtually ruled out by the fact that in the rest of the chapter when λαλέω refers to tongue-speaking it is invariably qualified by γλώσσῃ or γλώσσαις ('in a tongue' or 'in tongues'); λαλέω alone would not convey this specific reference.

and the mention of 'their own husbands' suggest that Paul's interest here is not in women in general, but in married women who were in some way behaving inappropriately? In that case the issue must relate to their 'desire to learn' something, which leads to the injunction to 'ask their husbands at home'. Because of the nature of the marriage relationship, it was not appropriate for the wife to act as spokesperson for the couple when they had a question to raise in the congregation. Because of the specific marriage terminology used, this may indeed be the special circumstance Paul has in mind, but the change of subject in the middle of a discussion of prophecy is still surprising. Perhaps some of the married women had been openly questioning what prophets (male or female, presumably) had said, and it was this which Paul felt to be a disruptive influence in worship. But it remains surprising that married women should be singled out for rebuke in this connection, unless of course it was their own husbands' prophetic utterances that they were challenging.

No-one finds 1 Corinthians 14.34–35 easy to explain in context. One of the best attempts I have come across, which incorporates the last two suggestions considered above into a reasonably plausible whole, is the following paraphrase by Kenneth Bailey:

> Women, please keep silent in worship and listen to the female and male prophets. Don't interrupt them with questions, and don't talk/chat in church. If you can't understand what is being said, ask your husbands at home. They understand more Greek than you do and will be able to explain things to you.[4]

But whatever the specific circumstance, it seems clear at least that these difficult verses, even if agreed to be by Paul, do not offer the basis for a general refusal to allow women any speaking role in any church, particularly in view of the fact that they occur in a letter which explicitly

---

4 K.E. Bailey, *Anvil* 11 (1994) 17. The suggestion concerning the better linguistic equipment of the husbands derives from the cosmopolitan nature of Corinth as a major sea-port, and the frequent tendency of immigrant women to be less exposed to the language than their working husbands. Bailey also adds an interesting parallel from Chrysostom who in the fourth century also suffered from noisy women's chatter during his sermons in the cathedral in Antioch!

documents the role of women in prophesying in the congregation.[5]

1 Timothy 2.8–15 – the storm-centre of debate

The unique importance of this passage for our subject lies especially in that: (1) it unambiguously addresses the respective roles of men and women when Christians come together to pray; (2) it explicitly prescribes the woman's role in relation to 'learning' and 'teaching' (rather than a more general term like 'speaking'); (3) the verb αὐθεντέω ('to have authority over'?) and the noun ὑποταγή ('submission') introduce the issue of the relationship of man and woman in terms of authority; (4) Paul's instruction is followed by a brief reference to the stories of Genesis 2–3 which suggests to some that it was for him a matter of theological principle rather than simply local expediency. No wonder, then, that it is on the exegesis of this passage that evangelical debates over the ordination of women are regularly centred.

The passage has, therefore, been extensively studied and discussed, not only in commentaries on 1 Timothy but also in a wide range of recent books which have aimed to set out a biblical approach to women's ministry.[6] Preeminent among these recent discussions must be the remarkably full (book-length) study by Richard and Catherine Kroeger[7] which not only goes into great detail on the various exegetical puzzles posed by the text, but does so in the context of a remarkably wide and well-informed survey of the relevant cultural background in Asia Minor in the first century. Those wishing for a more

---

5 For a much fuller study of the passage, taking account of a wide range of suggested interpretations, and concluding that these verses represent not a universal rule but a specific local problem of order, see Ben Witherington III, *Women in the Earliest Churches* (Cambridge: CUP, 1988) 90–104.

6 It would be tedious, and pointless, to list all such discussions. Studies specifically devoted to the exegesis of this passage which I have personally found particularly stimulating and informative have been D.M. Scholer in A. Mickelsen (ed), *Women, Authority and the Bible* (Downers Grove: IVP, 1986) 193–219; G.D.Fee, *Gospel and Spirit* (Peabody MA: Hendrickson, 1991) 52–65; K.E. Bailey, *Anvil* 11 (1994) 18–24.

7 R.C. and C.C. Kroeger, *I Suffer not a Woman: Rethinking 1 Timothy 2:11–15 in the Light of Ancient Evidence* (Grand Rapids: Baker, 1992).

satisfying study than can be presented in the space
available to me are warmly recommended to try the
Kroegers' book. But perhaps the smaller scope of this
chapter allows me the opportunity to offer an overview of
the issues which may whet the appetite.

The situation in Ephesus

In order to grasp the purpose and the significance of Paul's
injunctions with regard to the women at Ephesus, we
need to gain as clear a picture as possible of the situation
for which he was writing the letter. What was going on in
the Ephesian church which led him to instruct Timothy in
such stringent terms, and to lay down rules to which there
is no parallel in the rest of the New Testament?

There are two sources from which we may hope to gain
such information. We may ask the historians of ancient
Ephesus to give us a portrait of life, and particularly
religious life, in the city at that time. And we may also try,
with due caution, to infer from Paul's letter to Timothy
what sort of problems Timothy may have been encounter-
ing. If these two lines of enquiry converge on certain likely
areas of concern, we may be as close as we are likely to be
able to get to a realistic understanding of this controversial
text.

Ephesus, capital of the Roman province of Asia, was the
greatest commercial centre in Western Asia Minor, the
hub of commerce and travel in the area, and therefore the
location naturally chosen by Paul as the centre for his
work in the province (Acts 18.19 – 19.41; 20.16–38; 1 Cor.
16.8–9). Set up as a Greek colony, it became a rich,
cosmopolitan city where Greek and Asiatic culture were
inextricably mixed. Under the Roman emperors it became
inevitably the local centre for the imperial cult, but far
more important for its life and ethos was the temple of
'Artemis', the largest structure in the Hellenistic world,
and one of the Seven Wonders of the World. The huge
marble building, reputedly four times the size of the
Parthenon in Athens, had columns 65 feet high (the height
of a six-storey building); in the manner of a medieval
cathedral, it dominated the rest of the city. This temple
and its cult affected every aspect of the life of Ephesus and

the character of its society, and was the focus of a fierce civic pride (see Acts 19.23–41). For a whole month each year the city stopped work and devoted itself to the Artemis cult.[8]

Despite the Greek name by which she was known to the wider world, the goddess worshipped at Ephesus is not to be confused with Artemis, the virgin huntress of classical Greek mythology. She was the local tutelary deity, whose cult went back long before the arrival of the Greeks. While the central object of worship may have been a meteorite (the Διοπετής, literally 'fallen from heaven', Acts 19.35) the goddess herself was depicted in images which have survived from the Roman period as a mother-goddess with many breasts, a symbol of fertility. Her worship involved an enormous hierarchy of functionaries, headed by a group of eunuch-priests known as the *Megabyzoi*, under whom served both male and female priests, and notably some thousands of young women attendants. There is no clear evidence that cult prostitution was involved, though evidence of comparable cults elsewhere in Asia Minor suggests that it may have been.

The church of which Timothy had been put in charge lived in the shadow of this great temple, and can not have been unaffected by the surrounding atmosphere of a flamboyant and probably fairly uninhibited form of worship, in which women and eunuchs played a leading role. Just how this situation may have contributed to the problem faced in 1 Timothy 2.8–15 must be a matter of speculation. Kenneth Bailey paints the scene in strong colours:

> The focus of all this was a goddess whose worship was controlled by virgins who shared leadership with males only if they were castrated. In such an atmosphere what kind of female–male relations would have developed? What possibility would any male religious leadership have had for a sense of dignity and self-respect? What kind of female attitudes would have prevailed in such a city? . . . Castration being the ultimate violence against the male,

8 For an interesting recent account of the cult of Artemis at Ephesus, drawing on a wide range of scholarship, see C.E. Arnold, *Ephesians: Power and Magic* (Cambridge: CUP, 1989) 20–28; in keeping with his theme, Arnold draws particular attention to the links of the Artemis cult with magic and with the mystery religions.

would not anti-male sexism in various forms have been inevitable?[9]

Problems in the Ephesian church

Timothy, as Paul's representative in Ephesus, had an unenviable task. Paul needed to urge him to stay at his post in Ephesus (1.3), to 'fight the good fight' (1.18; 6.12), not to let anyone despise his youth (4.12). One has the impression of a man hanging on by his finger-tips in the hope that Paul will soon be able to return to relieve him (3.14–15; 4.13). His job is to resist and confute false teaching and irresponsible behaviour which apparently arises from within the church (1.3–7,19–20; 4.1–3,7,11–13; 5.20–22; 6.3–5,20–21). The situation is serious: some have already 'suffered shipwreck' (1.19) and 'missed the mark' (6.21), and it is only by Timothy's continued vigilance that he will save both himself and his hearers (4.16). The church is apparently in a parlous state, and Timothy himself seems not entirely sure that he has the resources to keep it from disaster.

What lay behind this serious concern of Paul's for the church in Ephesus? While some of the faults referred to in the letter are such as might be met in any young (or not so young!) church, there seem to have been certain more localised currents of teaching and behaviour which were particularly threatening.[10] We note the 'myths and endless genealogies' (1.4; cf 4.7), 'rejecting conscience' (1.19), 'forbidding marriage and demanding abstinence from foods' (4.3), 'a morbid craving for controversy and for dispute about words' (6.4), 'the profane chatter and contradictions of what is falsely called knowledge (γνῶσις)' (6.20). This last phrase has inevitably led to the identification of the trouble-makers as 'gnostics', and this may not be far wide of the mark so long as we do not imagine that there was in the first century a single definable religious movement called 'Gnosticism' with a fixed 'creed'. 'Gnostics' came in all shapes and sizes – the term is no more specific than 'New Age' is today, and indeed in some ways the two categories are not dissimilar. So perhaps Timothy

---

9 K.E. Bailey, *Anvil* 11 (1994) 19.
10 Note Paul's earlier warning to the elders of this same Ephesian church about the growth of false teaching from among their own number (Acts 20.29–30).

faced a local form of gnostic thought and teaching which, among other things, held ascetic views in relation to sex and food, presumably for the good gnostic reason that anything bodily is to be despised and all that counts is spiritual enlightenment.

Whatever name we give them, Timothy's opponents certainly degraded marriage (4.3). So it is not surprising that the relation between the sexes figures prominently in this letter, quite apart from 2.8–15. High among the qualifications required of a bishop are his marital status and family record (3.2,4–5); the same is also true of deacons (3.12); marriage is reaffirmed as a gift of God (4.3–5); Timothy's own dealings with women must be above reproach (5.2); and he is given detailed instructions on the pastoral care of widows (5.3–16), in the course of which their own record in marriage (5.9–10) and possible marriage prospects (5.11–14) are carefully considered. Marriage is, of course, an important aspect of any society or church, but the degree of attention given to it in this letter suggests that there was particular cause for concern in this area at Ephesus.

D.M. Scholer draws attention to this point as significant for the exegesis of 2.9–15. He suggests that rather than looking at the reference to child-bearing in 2.15 as a sort of appendix to Paul's argument, we should see it as the climax, and therefore allow it to influence our understanding of the whole passage. The problem, he suggests, was with women who were being influenced by this 'ascetic-gnosticizing movement within the church' to despise marriage and to aspire instead to roles in the life of the church for which they were not equipped. It is in the light of such a pastoral problem that Paul's advice to Timothy must be read. 'It addresses a particular situation of false teaching in Ephesus that assaulted and abused what was considered appropriate and honorable behavior for women.'[11]

In the light of this more general background we may note some of the terms and themes which occur specifically within 2.8–15. The focus on the physical appearance and dress of women in worship (vv. 9–10) reminds us of a similar passage in 1 Peter 3.3–6, where the issue is how

---

11 D.M. Scholer in A. Mickelsen (ed), *Women, Authority and the Bible*, 195–200 (quotation from p. 199).

Christian wives should commend their faith to their non-Christian husbands. The language of 'submission' in v. 11 reflects the same area of concern (as we saw in the last lecture), and we shall see shortly that the phrase οὐδὲ αὐθεντεῖν ἀνδρός ('not to have authority over a man') in v. 12 is probably better understood as demanding an appropriate relation between wife and husband (taking ἀνήρ in its more specific but very common sense of 'husband') than as relating more generally to the relation between women and men. Paul then appeals to the story of Adam and Eve, the paradigm 'married couple' (vv. 13–14), and the pericope ends with the commendation of child-bearing, the most distinctively 'wifely' role, as the proper and 'safe' way for the woman (v. 15). All this, taken with the striking focus on marriage in the rest of the letter, suggests strongly that Scholer is right, and that Paul's concern in these verses too is with the proper role for a wife in relation to her husband in the context of worship. If that is the case, there must be a question-mark against the use of this passage as a general prescription for the respective roles of men and women in worship, irrespective of the marriage relationship.

Another prominent feature of the letter as a whole is the importance of right teaching as a basis for right living. Timothy's primary role is to 'instruct certain people not to teach any different doctrine' (1.3), and references to the importance of sound teaching recur frequently (1.10–11; 3.2; 4.6,11,13,16; 5.17; 6.1–3). Timothy, as the one who has received the true teaching from Paul, is authorised to teach others; but he must resist those who set themselves up as teachers without due authority. Paul warns him specifically against those who 'desire to be teachers of the law, without understanding either what they are saying or the things about which they make assertions' (1.7). Clearly Timothy was confronted by ignorant would-be teachers.

This theme also emerges in our passage. The women (wives?) whom Paul forbids to teach in v. 12 are those who need first to 'learn' (v. 11). It is of course by no means a foregone conclusion in the ancient world that women would be encouraged to learn at all – that was men's role. But Paul wants them to learn. Until they have done so they are clearly not in a position to teach, but will come into the category of ignorant teachers condemned in 1.7. It is an interesting question whether when they have learned they would then be, in Paul's view, entitled to teach. Our passage does not answer that question, and commentators have, not surprisingly, answered it in different ways, depending on the view of women's ministry to which they are predisposed. But at least it must be admitted that the prohibition of women's teaching in 2.11 is in the context of their need to learn and of the danger posed in the church in Ephesus by unqualified teachers. Its application outside that context must be a matter of debate.

Some features of Paul's argument in 1 Timothy 2.8–15

In the light of this background awareness of the situation in Ephesus, we may now turn more directly to what Paul actually says about men and women in the church. At a number of points there are doubts either about the meaning of the terms used or about the way the argument is meant to be construed, but the contextual observations just offered may help us to decide which sense is most likely to have been intended in that situation. The passage may appropriately be considered in three sections.

1.   *Verses 8–10: Men and women at prayer*

The very first area of concern on which Paul instructs Timothy in this letter is the prayer life of the Ephesian church. In 2.1–7 Paul speaks about the subjects for prayer, and in 2.8–10 about the attitude and behaviour of men and women at prayer. It is out of these instructions that the controversial comments on the role of the women at Ephesus develop in vv. 11–15.

We should notice first that here, as often in the epistles, men and women are given their own separate instructions; there *is* a difference! Verse 9 begins with ὡσαύτως, 'likewise', which indicates that the reference to women's dress and demeanour is not changing to a new subject, but turning from how *men* should pray to specify how the women for their part are to pray. It is thus clear that here (as in 1 Corinthians 11) both sexes are assumed to be praying. The brief instruction to men concerns their attitude ('holy . . . without anger or argument'), while that to women is more specific and focuses (again as in 1 Corinthians 11) on their physical appearance as well as their behaviour. The parallel with 1 Corinthians 11 suggests that at Ephesus as at Corinth there was a tendency on the part of some women to behave in church in a 'liberated' way which was not conducive to true worship, and might be a scandal to others. In the light of the prevailing pagan context in Ephesus outlined above, we may perhaps infer that they were influenced by the freedom of the female-dominated worship of Artemis. Paul sees the danger of such an environment, and insists that in Christian worship the distinctive character of Christian women should be expressed in modesty of appearance and behaviour.

If this is the focus of Paul's concern, our understanding of the following instructions concerning women's 'teaching' and 'authority' should take this wider context into account.

2. Verses 11–12: Teaching and authority

These crucial verses contain three instructions concerning 'a woman' (or wife: γυνή, singular), and two nouns prescribing her attitude.

The one positive instruction is 'let her learn'. It is balanced by two negative instructions, 'not to teach' and 'not to have authority (αὐθεντεῖν) over a man (or her husband)'. The two nouns which describe the proper attitude are 'quietness (ἡσυχία)' and 'submission (ὑποταγή)'. Each of these five terms requires some discussion in this context.

'Let her learn'

We have noted above that Paul's encouragement to the women of the Ephesian church to learn would have seemed uncomfortably avant-garde to many in the ancient world. We have also noted the concern throughout 1 Timothy over false teaching within the church, which Paul attributes to sheer ignorance on the part of those who wished to be regarded as teachers (1.7). It may be, then, that the women whose 'liberated' behaviour in worship caused Paul to write vv. 9–10 may also have been among those claiming the status of teachers without first having learned the essentials of Christian truth. In such a situation it is notable that Paul does not simply prohibit these women from teaching, but also offers, indeed requires, the more positive alternative of learning. Those who must not teach are those who have yet to learn. The question of what their role will be when they have had the opportunity to learn does not yet arise at the time of Paul's writing, and so is not mentioned in the text.

'Not to teach'
The brief injunction does not indicate what type of teaching, or to what audience, Paul has in mind. It is remarkable how little this fact seems to worry those who oppose women's ordination. They assume that what is intended is the type of teaching associated by us with ordained ministry, and seem to have no difficulty in combining this prohibition with accepting that women should be school and university teachers, write authoritative books and present television documentaries, teach in Sunday Schools and Bible classes, and even carry the primary responsibility in missionary outreach and church-building in many non-Western contexts. Yet all these are 'teaching' roles, many of them involving men as the recipients of the teaching. Which of them, if any, did Paul have in mind? He does not say; the term he uses is broad and unspecific. Our chief clue must be again the concern of the letter as a whole with false teaching in the church, and there is no indication that such false teaching was confined to a formal 'pulpit' situation. It is likely that Christians in Ephesus met in quite small house churches, within which such false teaching easily spread. Such a scenario is suggested by 5.13, where we find some younger widows 'gadding about from house to house, . . . saying what they should not say'. Since, as we shall note later, there is a close parallel between the instructions given by Paul with regard to 'a woman' in 2.11–15 and those given with regard to the younger widows in 5.11–15,[12] this is perhaps the most natural focus in context for Paul's prohibition of a woman 'teaching'.

---

12 The parallel is analysed by G.D. Fee, *Gospel and Spirit*, esp. 57–58.

'Not to have authority over a man (or her husband)'
This instruction follows the requirement that the woman's
learning should be 'in all submission (ὑποταγή)', and the
two terms together suggest the wider Pauline concern for
a due 'order' within marriage, which was our subject in
the last chapter. But 'to have authority over' here
translates a rare Greek verb, αὐθεντέω, which Paul
nowhere else uses, and which is not found elsewhere in
the New Testament. Had he wished to speak about
'authority' in the normal sense he could have used a more
regular Greek verb, such as προίστημι (which he uses of
authority in both home and church in 3.4–5,12; 5.17) or the
noun ἐξουσία. What then is the special connotation of
αὐθεντέω which causes him to prefer such an unusual verb
here? On the sparse evidence of non-biblical Greek usage,
it is often suggested that there is a pejorative tone to
αὐθεντέω, as was assumed by the Authorised Version
rendering, 'to usurp authority over'; cf. NEB 'domineer
over', REB 'dictate to'. This pejorative element is suggested
not so much on the basis of the usage of the verb itself, but
from the cognate noun αὐθέντης, which is defined by
Liddell and Scott as 'one who does anything with his own
hand', and in particular a murderer. In an ancient
commentary on Aeschylus the verb also is clearly used to
mean 'commit murder', but this is an exceptional use.[13] A
detailed study by George Knight has argued that in
general the verb carries the sense of authority with no
necessarily pejorative overtones.[14] On the other hand
Kenneth Bailey[15] has noted that ancient Syriac and Arabic
versions of 1 Timothy understand the verb as implying
'insolence and bullying', 'to be domineering', 'to be
imperious',[16] and on this basis suggests that the Ephesian

---

13 Note, however, that R.C. and C.C. Kroeger, *I Suffer not a Woman* 185–188,
discuss seriously the possibility, in the light of the background in mystery
religions and in gnostic thought, that the term might actually be used in 1 Tim.
2.12 with reference to 'actual or representational murder'.
14 George W. Knight III, 'Αὐθεντέω in Reference to Women in 1 Timothy 2.12',
NTS 30 (1984) 143–157. Knight surprisingly chooses not to include the one
admittedly pejorative use (in the sense of 'commit murder') in his tabulation of
uses because it 'helps little with the 1 Timothy 2.12 passage' (p. 144); he might
better have left this for the reader to judge.
15 K.E. Bailey, *Anvil* 11 (1994) 21.
16 The Vulgate *dominari in virum* may probably have a similarly pejorative
connotation, though the usage of the verb is too wide to allow certainty on this.

women were 'brutalizing' the men; he offers the paraphrase 'I do not allow these ignorant women to batter the
men. They are to stop shouting and calm down'. Here is
another debate which is not likely to be settled definitiv-
ely, given the scarcity of the verb. Certainly Paul forbids a
woman to exercise authority over a man (or her husband),
but the question whether he refers to any authority at all,
or more specifically to a misused, usurped authority,
remains unresolved. If he intended to say that no woman
may ever be in a position where she has authority over a
man, he has chosen an unnecessarily obscure way to say
it!

'Quietness and submission'
I have deliberately used 'quietness' rather than 'silence' to
translate ἡσυχία, since when Paul (if it is Paul!) calls on the
Corinthian women to be silent he uses the normal verb for
silence, σιγάω. Here he has chosen to use twice over the
wider term ἡσυχία, which refers not primarily to absence of
speech or noise, but to 'quietness' of temperament. This
noun does not therefore contain a prohibition of speech
(it is the command 'not to teach' which, in some sense,
conveys that), but a commendation of a restful, unargu-
mentative attitude. As such it coheres well with the call for
'submission', which we have seen in the last chapter to be
the proper attitude of a Christian wife according to Pauline
and other New Testament teaching. If αὐθεντέω is
understood in the more pejorative sense, then both ἡσυχία
and ὑποταγή are its natural opposites.
   Verses 11–12 therefore leave a lot of questions unresolved. 'A woman' (or wife) is instructed to learn and not
to teach, to be quiet and submissive and not to exercise (an
improper?) authority over a man (or her husband). We do
not know exactly what it was in current church practice in
Ephesus which evoked this instruction, nor is it clear how
far it is intended to relate to the Ephesian women in
general and how far only to the relationship between a
married couple. Quite apart from the question of what
relevance Paul's words might be expected to have outside
the specific situation for which he was writing, we have to
admit that even within that situation his words remain (to
us, but presumably not to the original readers) open to
various interpretations.

3. Verses 13–15: Adam and Eve, and childbirth

What gives 1 Timothy 2.8–15 special prominence in the debate about the role of women in ministry is the frequently repeated assertion that Paul derives his argument from a 'creation principle', thus making it clear that this is not simply a local prescription for one particular problem situation, but rests on the permanent God-given order of things. That is at least a questionable assertion.

He does not say that he is appealing to a 'creation principle'. The reference to Adam and Eve is introduced by the simple conjunction 'for'. This conjunction encourages his readers to think back to the account of man and woman in Genesis 2 and 3 (not to the primary creation account in Genesis 1, where man-and-woman are created together and given authority jointly over the rest of creation). There, in contrast to the first creation account, they will find that Adam was created first, but it was the woman who took the lead in yielding to temptation. How then does this observation relate to the instruction given in vv. 11–12?

If the logic is simply that the first to be created must necessarily be the superior, one might wonder why human beings are not subject to the rest of the animal creation. If it is that the woman was responsible for the entry of sin and therefore women are inevitably the source of sin and false teaching, why does Paul argue in Romans 5 that sin came through the transgression of Adam, with no mention of Eve? If he is arguing that women cannot be trusted with authority because Eve's example shows that they are inherently more gullible (a generalisation which is not always verified by experience!), in what sense is this a 'creation principle'? (It might better be called a 'fall principle', and that would raise interesting questions about its validity in the era of redemption!)

Again we are confronted by a brief, enigmatic comment by Paul which is very variously interpreted. The mere fact that it refers to Adam and Eve does not make it a 'creation principle'. It is an illustration from a well-known text of a danger inherent in the relationship between men and women. In the story of Genesis 2 and 3 we see an example of a woman who took the initiative, with disastrous consequences. Created after Adam to be his 'helper', she instead acted independently and listened to the tempter. She thus illustrates the way some of the Ephesian women were behaving, asserting their independence and open to be deceived by false teaching. In such a situation, they must be denied the right to teach or hold authority; they need, as Eve needed, rather to learn in all submission.

This is an intelligible, if cryptic, argument by way of an example drawn from the Genesis narrative, but to dignify it with the title of a 'creation principle' is to suggest a level of theological deliberation and of universal application which the context does not support.[17]

The continuation of the argument in v. 15 seems only to deepen the obscurity of the argument and to widen the range of interpretations on offer! I have long been attracted by the suggestion that this reference to childbirth develops the mention of Eve's sin by referring to the curse of Genesis 3.16. Childbirth, blighted and dangerous since the fall, can nonetheless be safe – a good Christian wife 'will be *brought safe through* childbirth'. But it must be recognised that Paul does not elsewhere use σῴζω ('save') in its gospels sense of physical well-being. Nor does 'safe childbirth' seem a particularly apposite idea in this context; it makes the verse into a largely irrelevant appendix.

It may indeed be the thought-connection between the story of the fall and Genesis 3.16 that leads Paul in this context to mention childbirth, but in a context where the first sin has just been mentioned it seems most unlikely that σῴζω refers to anything but spiritual salvation (especially since Paul has prominently raised that very issue in vv. 3–7). In that case, if we dismiss as contrived (as I believe we must) the proposal that 'the Childbirth' is an obscure way of referring to the incarnation of Christ,

---

17 A large part of the Kroegers' book (*I Suffer not a Woman*, pp. 117–170) is devoted to arguing that vv. 13–14 are intended to refute a widespread gnostic veneration of Eve. They show that in gnostic mythology Eve had become the first to be created, and was revered as the original source of enlightenment (γνῶσις), and they produce abundant evidence that such ideas would have been current in first-century Ephesus. Eve had thus become the symbol of the Ephesian women's claim to precedence in the church, and it is therefore necessary for Paul to refute their claims as based on a false mythology (cf 1.4; 4.7), not on the Genesis account itself. If this is a valid understanding of vv. 13–14, Paul's motive in referring to the Genesis stories is even further removed from the supposed establishment of a 'creation principle' as the basis of his instructions in vv. 11–12.

Paul is in some way linking the spiritual salvation of these women to their fulfilment of the normal wifely role of bearing children, provided that their lifestyle is also in other ways appropriate ('faith, love, holiness, modesty'). Uncomfortable as this may be for a Protestant doctrine of salvation by faith not works, it is more easily understood if we remember that one of the heresies of the false teachers at Ephesus was the prohibition of marriage (4.3). If we are to imagine a 'super-spiritual' asceticism which despised marriage and childbirth and invited Christian women to the sort of spiritual liberation which had resulted in the behaviour Paul is trying to curb in vv. 9–12, then it is easily understandable that Paul should insist that the way of salvation is rather to be found in the normal married relationship and in the child-bearing which is the most distinctively feminine part of it.

In that case, far from being an irrelevant appendix, v. 15 is the climax of an appeal to the Ephesian women to abandon the heady new 'gnostic' idea of a liberated role in teaching and worship, for which in their ignorant state they are totally unfitted, and to return to the wholesome normality of a Christian marriage relationship, within which 'quietness' amd 'submission' replace the premature grasp for a role of authority in the church.

Preliminary conclusions on 1 Timothy 2.8–15

The preceding paragraphs do not claim to have set out a full exegesis of this complex passage. I have suggested some aspects of the situation in Ephesus which may affect how we understand it, and in looking at the content of Paul's argument I have tried to keep these background features in mind, and to set out some of the exegetical options.

I do not claim that my discussion has been even-handed. I suspect that a non-partisan study of this passage would be very hard to find – and if it existed the sheer range of possibilities on offer would make it both tedious and frustrating. Certainly those exegetical studies of the passage which I have seen written by those who hold a more restricted view of women's ministry have been no less partisan.

We have to admit that we know too little about the

circumstances of the letter, and that there are too many obscure or ambiguous features to the argument, to allow any exegesis to claim to have uttered the last word. But that conclusion is in itself important for our present theme. This is, by common consent, the one passage of Scripture on which the argument against the ordination of women rests most firmly. If even this pivotal passage proves to be open to such a range of interpretation, and to leave so many unresolved questions for the modern interpreter, how secure a basis can it be for resolving an issue of major ecclesiological importance?

It is a good rule to interpret Scripture in the light of Scripture, and to interpret the more obscure in the light of the clearer. The above discussion suggests that 1 Timothy 2.8–15 (no less than 1 Corinthians 14.34–35) falls rather firmly into the category of the more obscure! In the next chapter I shall therefore aim to set these difficult texts in the wider context of the New Testament (and indeed of the whole Bible), in the hope that their exegetical puzzles may be to some extent clarified by the fuller biblical witness.

But one further point remains to be made, more fundamental than all that I have said so far. In this chapter I have been engaged in exegesis, attempting as best I could to elucidate what Paul meant and why he said it at the time. Inevitably my exegetical decisions have been coloured by my own viewpoint, and will be open to debate for that reason. But I have deliberately attempted to stay within the first century context, and have avoided so far raising the question of the relevance of Paul's words to another time and place. Yet it is this latter question which is ultimately the most important for our purposes. It would be possible to conclude that Paul had no objection to the ministry of women but that it should not be exercised in our own situation today – or that Paul totally forbade it as a matter of principle but that his instructions apply only to his own context, not to our very different world. In other words, even if we could have solved the exegetical questions to the satisfaction of all concerned, the hermeneutical decisions, and with them the possibility of disagreement, still remain.

There are aspects of Paul's instructions to Timothy which few modern Christians would regard as binding on the church today. Even within our own passage, Paul prohibits the braiding of hair and the wearing of gold, pearls and expensive clothes (v. 9), yet I know of few modern church circles, however committed to the authority of Scripture, where these prohibitions are regarded as mandatory. Yet they are part of the same paragraph in which Paul also prohibits women to teach and hold authority. On what basis are the two parts of his instructions treated differently?

The same observation relates to 1 Corinthians 11.2–16, with its rules on women's head-covering. We have noted the similarity between the situations in Corinth and Ephesus, and the likelihood that Paul is here motivated by a similar concern to prevent women in the congregation from exploiting their new liberty in Christ in inappropriate ways. The rules laid down in 1 Corinthians 11.2–16 are widely regarded within Western Christendom as no longer literally applicable; why then should the similar rules of 1 Timothy 2.8–15 be given any more universal status?

Gordon Fee[18] points out a further interesting parallel within 1 Timothy. He notes a very close similarity between the instructions given to 'a woman' in 2.9–15 and his instructions for the conduct of younger widows in 5.11–15:

> Rather than displaying the 'good works' of the older widows, which includes rearing children well (5.10), they have apparently 'given themselves to pleasure' (v. 6), have grown wanton against Christ in their desire to remarry (v. 12; apparently outside the faith). Furthermore, they have become busybodies, going about from house to house (house-church to house-church?) talking foolishness and speaking of things they should not (v. 13; the false teachings? cf. the description of the false teachers in 1.6–7). As such they have already gone astray after Satan (v. 15). Paul's solution here is for them to remarry (vis-à-vis the false teachers; cf. 4.3) and bear children, so as not to give the enemy cause to reproach the gospel (v. 14).
> The concern and solution in 2.9–15 are nearly identical. . . .

Yet, as Fee rightly points out, these verses have not been the focus of much attention in the modern church. The issue of how widows should be treated was so important

---

18 G.D. Fee, *Gospel and Spirit*, pp. 57–58.

to Paul that he devoted the whole of 5.3-16 to it (much more space than is devoted to the role of women in chapter 2), yet modern Christians seem to have no difficulty in relegating this section to the area of merely historical interest, rules for a bygone situation which can have no direct bearing on our modern society. On what basis, then, is his concern over the behaviour of the Ephesian women at prayer of any more ultimate significance or more literally applicable to modern church life?

I do not suggest that the answer to these questions is simple, nor do I expect that all will agree on them. But it does seem to me important that they should be raised and debated. Most of those who claim permanent normative authority for 2.8–15 simply assume that it is in some way of more permanent relevance than the rules for widows, but such inconsistency of hermeneutical approach needs to be defended rather than assumed. It is, of course, sometimes defended on the basis that Paul here offers a 'creation principle', but we have seen reason to doubt the validity of that claim. Here, as so often in Paul's letters, he is dealing with a specific local situation, some of the contours of which I have tried to outline above. How far, and in what way, his instructions for Timothy in that situation in Ephesus can be extrapolated to other areas of church life must be a matter for argument, not for tacit assumption. As Gordon Fee comments, 'It is hard to deny that *this* text prohibits women teaching men in the Ephesian church; but it is the unique text in the New Testament, and as we have seen, its reason for being is *not* to correct the rest of the New Testament, but to correct a very ad hoc problem in Ephesus.'[19]

We turn, then, in the next chapter, to see what light the rest of the New Testament may throw on the role of women in the apostolic church.

---

19 G.D. Fee, *Gospel and Spirit*, pp. 63–64.

CHAPTER FOUR

Women in the New Testament Church – and in the Church Today:
Continuity and Development

In the first chapter I explored the relevance of biblical
hermeneutics to evangelical disagreements over the ordination of women, with special reference to the priesthood of the Church of England. I pointed out that the
opposite conclusions to which evangelicals have come on
the issue can both be presented as the legitimate application of biblical teaching, that the division is not one over
the authority of Scripture, but over the right way to
interpret and apply it. I suggested that the conflicting
views derived from two different hermeneutical
approaches, the one focusing on certain passages and
strands of the New Testament which suggest that there is
a permanent God-given distinction between the roles of
men and women which rules out the exercise of teaching
and authority by women, while the other appeals to the
wider scriptural pattern and also questions whether
apostolic rulings for first-century church situations should
be applied in the same way to the very different church
scene of twentieth-century Europe.

The second and third chapters examined the New
Testament evidence most commonly cited by those
opposed to the ordination of women. In the second
chapter I discussed the apostolic principle that there is a
priority within the marriage relationship which requires
the wife to 'submit' to the husband, but questioned how
far this distinction between the sexes can be applied

outside the context of marriage. I noted, however, that one of Paul's two uses of the metaphor of the man as 'head' of the woman occurs in a passage (1 Cor. 11.2–16) which is not specifically talking about marriage, but rather about the behaviour of women and men in church. But that passage, far from forbidding women to take an active role in worship, specifically recognises their participation through prophecy and prayer. What it does in fact explicitly prohibit is that women should worship with heads uncovered, a rule which neither side in the current debate seems keen to regard as of permanent literal application!

In the third chapter we considered briefly the command for women to be silent in church in 1 Corinthians 14.34–35 and at greater length the key passage 1 Timothy 2.8–15, where Paul forbids a woman to teach or hold authority over a man (or her husband). Apart from the question of the authenticity of the 1 Corinthians passage as part of Paul's original letter, both passages proved to involve considerable difficulties, and room for disagreement, even at the exegetical level of deciding just what the author meant and why he wrote as he did in that particular situation. Neither therefore seemed to offer the firm basis for decision which is sometimes claimed, and the suggestion that in 1 Timothy 2.13–15 Paul grounds his ruling in a 'creation principle' was found to be at least dubious. Moreover, the further and fundamental question of how Paul's rulings for the first-century problems of the Corinthian and Ephesian churches, even if we could fully understand them in their own context, may most appropriately be applied to the very different situation of twentieth-century Britain, and of priesthood in the Church of England, still remains to be answered.

In the light of all this, I turn in this final chapter to the alternative hermeneutical approach outlined in the first chapter, and aim to set the more specific passages and themes so far discussed within the wider context of the developing place of women in the Old and New Testaments. I shall focus in particular on the evidence of the New Testament that even within the first-century churches their role was by no means so restricted as 1 Timothy 2.11–12 might suggest.

Women in the Old Testament

Old Testament Israel was a patriarchal society, in which a man's wife could be listed along with his servants and animals, and after his house, as part of his possessions (Ex. 20.17), and in which a woman was always under the authority of a man, whether father, brother or husband.[1] In such a society all cultic and political offices were inevitably held by men. There were no women priests, and the only queen to hold office in Judah is presented as a usurper, at whose overthrow 'all the people of the land rejoiced' (2 Ki. 11.1–20). As in any patriarchal society, however, there were of course influential women, who knew how to wield power within the male-dominated structure (notably, and in very different ways, Jezebel and Esther).

From time to time a woman arose who held a recognised position of leadership, though this was normally in a prophetic role, rather than by holding any formal office. Miriam, who had an influential though subordinate place alongside Moses and Aaron in the Exodus period, is described as a prophet (Ex. 15.20). Deborah was a prophetess, and is even described as 'judging Israel' (Jdg. 4.4–5), though the narrative makes it clear that, in battle if not in civil administration, it was Barak who took the formal lead at Deborah's instigation. Huldah (also a prophetess) was apparently the natural authority for the king's officials to consult when sent to 'enquire of the Lord' on a matter of state importance (2 Ki. 22.12–20). A prophetess, Noadiah, was among Nehemiah's political challengers (Neh. 6.14). Other references to women prophets indicate no sense that women as such should not prophesy, even though women prophets, no less than male ones, could be in error (Ezek. 13.17ff; Joel 2.28f). There were also 'wise women' in Israel, distinct from prophetesses, who exercised considerable influence among their people (2 Sam. 14.1–20; 20.16–22).

Old Testament society therefore differed little from the patriarchal model which characterised most societies of the period, though the Old Testament narratives provide

---

1 The permission, in the case of Zelophehad's daughters, for women to inherit in the absence of a male heir (Num. 27.1–11; 36.1–12) is the exception which proves the rule.

some evidence that women, even if they held no formal office, could sometimes be recognised as speaking with divine authority or wisdom, and through this endowment could on occasion exercise significant and even leading roles in society.

Women in the ministry of Jesus

Society had changed little in this respect by the time of Jesus; indeed it seems likely that the development of rabbinic legislation was making it more difficult rather than easier for women to play any prominent role. Numerous rabbinic sayings and stories, even if codified later than the time of Jesus, clearly reflect a culture in which a sage could advise his pupils to 'talk not much with womankind' (Mishnah, *Aboth* 1.5), in which when a man and a woman were in danger of death, the man must be saved first (Mishnah, *Horayoth* 3.7) and in which even the great Rabbi Judah could without embarrassment instruct every man in daily worship (and in the presence of women) to thank God that he had not been created a Gentile, a woman, or an illiterate (Tosefta, *Berakoth* 7.18; Babylonian Talmud, *Menahoth* 43b). The words of the Torah are better burned than handed to a woman (Jerusalem Talmud, *Sotah* 10a). In Herod's temple, unlike the Old Testament places of worship, there was a 'Court of the Women' marking the limit beyond which only men could go to worship near the holy place, and at least by the end of the first century women were segregated from men in synagogue worship. Josephus sums it up in the statement, 'The woman is in all things inferior to the man' (*Apion* 2.201). The picture was not uniform, of course, and examples can be found of a more enlightened attitude, which allowed women to be taught the Law and even to have a limited role in worship.[2] But such instances stand out simply because they are unusual.

In the gospels we meet Anna the prophetess (Lk. 2.36–38), a well-known figure in the temple, but apparently

---

2 See Ben Witherington III, *Women and the Genesis of Christianity* (Cambridge: CUP, 1990) 3–9 for an unusually positive account of the status of women in Judaism. For a very full and far less optimistic account see J. Jeremias, *Jerusalem in the Time of Jesus* (London: SCM, 1969) 359–376; cf. A. Oepke, *TDNT* 1, 781–784.

without any official status, still less any role of religious leadership. And within the group who gathered around Jesus it was men who occupied the leading roles, notably the twelve. Yet it is important to note that the wider circle of Jesus' followers was not, as rabbinic precedent might have led us to expect, made up only of men. When Jesus contrasts his natural family with the disciple group, the latter is appropriately described as 'my mother and brothers', but its inclusive nature is then emphasised by the further phrase 'my brother and sister and mother' (Mt. 12.48–50; Mk. 3.33–35). Some of these 'sisters' are named in Luke 8.1–3, and it is remarkable that Mary, Joanna, Susanna and the others are described not just as supporters but as travelling companions who were 'with Jesus' in the same way as the twelve; such a mixed itinerant group would have stood out as at least unusual, if not potentially scandalous, in the light of rabbinic practice.

It is, of course, entirely in character that Jesus should have been prepared to challenge the cultural norm in this way. The records of his ministry are full of contacts with the outcast and unrespectable, and in particular include many encounters with women, whom he seems to have treated as deserving his attention on a par with men. They are not merely the passive recipients of his miraculous power and his pastoral care (Mk. 1.29–31; 5.21–43; Lk. 7.36–50; 13.11–17 etc), but can on occasion be engaged in serious theological dialogue (Mt. 15.21–28; Jn. 4.7–29). Jesus rebuked his (male) disciples for their objections to a woman's extravagant devotion, and declared that the story would continue to be told 'in remembrance of her' (Mk. 14.3–9; cf Mk. 12.41–44). When Mary opted for the more 'male' role of disciple over against Martha's more traditional understanding of the woman's task, Jesus unambiguously took her side (Lk. 10.38–42).

All this adds up to an attitude quite out of keeping with traditional Jewish attitudes and particularly with the ethos of the rabbinic writings. Women were not, for Jesus, mere possessions of men, or even second-class citizens; still less were they primarily of sexual interest. He related to women and valued them as real people of independent worth and personality, and they played a significant role in the movement which arose out of his public ministry. It may seem surprising in that case that no women were included among the twelve, but it may fairly be replied that the choice of the twelve (like the designation of Peter as the Rock on which the church was built) was a historical provision of limited duration, not an ideological statement about the permanent values of the kingdom of God. In the cultural context of the time it was perhaps inevitable that men should form the inner circle around Jesus, but Luke 8.1–3 suggests that that inner circle was not very sharply distinguished in practice from the wider group of companions among whom women were prominent.

When Jesus' ministry came to its climax in Jerusalem the importance of the women in his entourage became clear. When the (male) disciples abandoned Jesus to his fate, it was the women who remained at the cross, who witnessed the burial of his body, who looked after its ritual needs, and who therefore were the only ones in a position to be the first witnesses of his resurrection. In a society which did not recognise women as legally acceptable witnesses, it was women who were commissioned to bear witness to the empty tomb (and who met at first with the predictably dismissive response of the Jewish male, Lk. 24.10–11!).

The gospels do not, perhaps, record a total reversal of Jewish prejudice against women and of their exclusion from roles of leadership. But they do contain the seeds from which such a reversal was bound to grow. Effective revolutions are seldom completed in a year or two. In this, as in other matters, the disciples were slow learners. But the fuse, long as it might prove to be, had been ignited. In the ministry of Jesus we see an irreversible turning of the wheel which set the Jesus movement on a new course with regard to the respective roles of men and women.

Women in the apostolic church

Much of our knowledge of the first-century Christian churches derives from the letters of Paul, to which we shall turn shortly. But Luke's account of the apostolic church in Acts yields some interesting indications of the role women played among the first Christians. Just as in Luke 8.1–3 he has associated women with the twelve as

Jesus' travelling companions, so in Acts 1.13–14 he lists the eleven remaining apostles as meeting in Jerusalem 'together with certain women, including Mary the mother of Jesus, as well as his brothers'. The 'headquarters' of Jesus' disciples in the immediate post-Easter period therefore contains both men and women. From that point on, Luke is careful to mention repeatedly that the converts won in the early days included both men and women (Acts 5.14; 8.3; 9.2; 17.34), and sometimes stresses the social prominence of the women converts (Acts 17.4,12).

One important role played by Christian women in Acts, as in Luke's gospel, is the provision of premises and hospitality for the disciple group. In Jerusalem they met in the house of Mary the mother of John Mark (perhaps a widow?, Acts 12.12), and here, as at the empty tomb, the message of God's work of deliverance is entrusted to a woman (indeed to a slave woman), who meets with similar disbelief on the part of the disciples (Acts 12.13–17).

In Philippi it was Lydia, the first convert in Europe and a successful business-woman, who provided hospitality for the infant church (Acts 16.14–15,40); indeed Lydia appears in the Acts narrative as the leading member of the Philippian church, and it is interesting that when Paul later wrote to this same church women still played a leading role in it (Phil. 4.2–3). The cultural context in Macedonia probably provided an environment in which it was more widely acceptable for women to play a prominent role than it would have been in Judaea, and Paul seems to have exploited this openness effectively. Luke's account suggests that the church began with Paul's preaching to a riverside gathering consisting entirely of women of Jewish sympathies; the first male convert comes later (Acts 16.27–34).

Among other women who come to the fore in Luke's story are Tabitha, 'devoted to good works and acts of charity' (Acts 9.36–42), and the four daughters of Philip who were recognised as prophetesses (Acts 21.9). It is intriguing that Luke pointedly describes Philip's daughters also as 'virgins', so that there may be in his mind some connection between their marital condition and their role of prophecy. Ben Witherington comments, 'It is probably not coincidental that most of the women we find in Acts playing a significant role were either single or widowed'.[3] Is there a suggestion here that there was more freedom for Christian ministry on the part of the unmarried, who were not expected to be 'in submission' to a husband?

But the woman who is most prominently mentioned in Acts was certainly married. The couple Priscilla and Aquila appear in Acts 18.2,18,26, as well as (in the form Prisca rather than Priscilla) in Romans 16.3; 1 Corinthians 16.19; 2 Timothy 4.19. They were prominent among Paul's fellow-workers, widely known among the first-century churches (Rom. 16.3–4), and hosted the local church (1 Cor. 16.19; Rom. 16.5). In Acts they appear first as Paul's hosts (and fellow-tentmakers) at Corinth, and then as his travelling-companions as far as Ephesus. But they are soon back in Corinth, in Paul's absence, and take the initiative in 'taking aside' the formidable Apollos and teaching him a 'more accurate' version of the Christian message than he had yet encountered (Acts 18.26). Clearly they were a force to be reckoned with in early Mediterranean Christianity!

It is unusual for a couple to be mentioned together in this way; neither of them is ever mentioned alone. But even more remarkable is the fact that after the socially correct introduction of the couple in Acts 18.2 with Aquila's name preceding that of his wife, Luke thereafter mentions them in the opposite order, as does Paul in both Romans 16.3 and 2 Timothy 4.19. It is hard to avoid the conclusion that within this husband-and-wife team it was Priscilla who was the more noticeable partner and whose ministry was particularly important for the growth of the church. That a Jewish woman should be recorded as taking the lead in giving religious instruction to the the Jewish teacher Apollos, 'an eloquent man, well-versed in the Scriptures', is, by contemporary Jewish standards, quite astounding – and Paul's evident approval of her activity is very hard to square with the traditional interpretation of 1 Timothy 2.11–12 as forbidding any woman ever to teach or have authority over a man![4]

---

3 Ben Witherington III, *Women in the Earliest Churches*, 152.
4 It is an interesting testimony to the significance of Priscilla in the New Testament that her name has been seriously proposed as the author of the (anonymous) Letter to the Hebrews, notably by Adolf Von Harnack.

The early church as it appears in Acts remained a male-dominated movement, but one within which the seeds of greater equality of the sexes and a more prominent role for women which we saw planted in Jesus' ministry were beginning to grow. Particularly as the church moved outside the firmly Jewish cultural context of Palestine, the situation began to change, even though the leading figures in this development (Paul, Priscilla, Aquila, Apollos etc.) were themselves Jewish, and the first focus of evangelism remained the Jewish community in the Diaspora. In Priscilla at least we find a growth of female leadership in the church, with Paul's full approval, which does not fit the stereotype of a church which had no place for women in positions of authority.

Women in the Pauline churches

In the previous chapters we noted a few passages in the Pauline letters which indicate that he needed to curb the enthusiasm and insensitivity of women in the churches of Corinth and Ephesus. The fact that such curbs were needed is itself significant: churches where women knew that they could expect no role in leadership or public speaking would not be likely to require such restraint. It was the freedom women now felt to be open to them in Christ, such as the right to pray or prophesy which Paul recognises in 1 Corinthians 11.5, which led some of them into inappropriate behaviour and thus required Paul's corrective action. Other incidental references in Paul's letters also indicate that in fact the role of women in the Christian churches was much less constrained than the popular stereotype allows.

The most focused discussion of the relation between men and women in Paul's letters is 1 Corinthians 7. Its subject-matter is marriage and singleness, and so it is not likely to contribute directly to our theme of women's role in the church's ministry. It is worth noting, however, that the focus of discussion in this chapter is not, as in some other Pauline passages, on the issue of authority and submission within marriage, but rather on the equality of man and woman with regard to sexual rights and responsibilities. Frequently through the chapter he is careful to balance what he says about one sex with a parallel statement about the other, even including the remarkable statement that the wife 'has authority over' the husband's body (note vv. 2–5, 10–11, 12–16, 28, 32–34); this is a far cry from traditional Jewish teaching where marriage was all about a man's rights and responsibilities, with no parallel concern for the woman. Within this context, Paul's concern emerges that women should be free from the other anxieties which marriage brings, in order to be able the better to concentrate on 'the affairs of the Lord' (v. 34). He goes on to speak especially of the pursuit of holiness in body and spirit, but it is at least worth considering whether he may not have some more specific service in mind, since presumably holiness would be expected of married women as well. Just what role was open to the unmarried woman which was not so readily fulfilled by the married he does not say. But that he should consider the single state as one of positive value, rather than as an unfortunate failure to fulfil woman's true role as wife and mother, is a significant departure from traditional Jewish thinking, and one which opens the way for a more positive approach to women's ministry in the church.

The references to the activity of women in worship in the rest of 1 Corinthians have already been discussed in the previous two chapters. We noted there the uneasy tension between the acceptance that women might appropriately pray and prophesy in church (1 Cor. 11.5) and the demand that they be silent (1 Cor. 14.34–35), leading some scholars to take more seriously than might otherwise have been the case the textual indications that 1 Corinthians 14.34–35 may not have been part of the original letter. We noted too the concept of the man as 'head' of the woman (1 Cor. 11.3), and the question whether this metaphor can appropriately be applied generally to the respective roles of men and women in worship, or whether it applies only to the marriage relationship (as it clearly does in Eph. 5.23).

But more clearly relevant to our purposes than these enigmatic instructions derived from the internal problems of the Corinthian church are the indications from Paul's letters of the role women were actually playing within the churches with which he was associated. Not that Paul ever offers a formal description of women's ministry in these young churches – that would be too much to hope for in a collection of occasional letters which were written not to set out a systematic theology nor to describe the prevalent pattern of church government and ministry, but simply to deal with pastoral issues which had arisen in specific situations. What they do offer us is unintended glimpses, through Paul's brief comments on individual colleagues and friends, of what Christian women were actually doing in his churches. But perhaps that is just what we need, not a conscious argument by Paul for or against women's ministry, but the artless disclosure of what was in fact going on. Such evidence, precisely because it is so unselfconscious, gives us a more secure historical background against which to interpret the controversial passages in Paul's letters.

One such snapshot is in Paul's letter to Philippi, a church which, as we have seen, seems from its foundation to have depended to a significant degree on its women members, particularly Lydia. One of Paul's pastoral concerns for this church is apparently to resolve a dispute between two of its leading members, Euodia and Syntyche (Phil. 4.2–3). These two women are described as people who 'have struggled beside me in the work of the gospel, together with Clement and the rest of my co-workers'. Paul does not describe them by any more official title, so that we can only surmise whether, in addition to being recognised as evangelists, 'strugglers' in the work of the gospel, they were also among the ἐπίσκοποι καὶ διάκονοι (traditionally translated 'bishops and deacons') to whom in particular Paul and Timothy sent their greetings (Phil. 1:1). But to be counted among Paul's 'co-workers' and his fellow-'strugglers' in the work of the gospel suggests a role of considerable responsibility and authority. Their disagreement was sufficiently important to the well-being of the whole church to make it necessary for Paul to tackle it openly in a public letter. Paul mentions only three of his 'co-workers' at Philippi by name, and two of those three are women. While the immediate reason for these two to be mentioned is their recent bad relationship, this nonetheless suggests that women played a significant role in the 'leadership team' of that church.

But we are not told explicitly whether Euodia and Syntyche were among the ἐπίσκοποι καὶ διάκονοι of the

Philippian church. We shall, however, see shortly in Romans 16 that the titles of διάκονος ('deacon') and ἀπόστολος ('apostle') were in fact applied by Paul to two of his women colleagues. It has also been argued that in 1 Timothy there is a mention of women elders (a title generally understood to be roughly equivalent to the term ἐπίσκοπος which Paul uses in Phil. 1.1, and of course in 1 Tim. 3.1–7; Tit. 1.7–9). Kenneth Bailey[5] argues that in 1 Timothy 5.1 the term πρεσβύτερος, normally translated 'an older man', should be translated 'an elder', and that the following πρεσβυτέρας would then naturally mean not 'older women' but 'women elders'. He argues this on the basis of a structural analysis of 1 Timothy 4.6 – 5.22 as an inverted parallelism, within which 4.12 – 5:2 and 5.17–20 are parallel discussions of 'Timothy and the elders'. This translation is certainly possible, and it would be wrong to allow our exegesis to be determined by a contrary tradition which reflects the presuppositions of a later church which did not recognise women elders. But the presence of references to 'younger men' and 'younger women' in the same verse suggests to me at least that the traditional rendering is in this case in itself more likely, and that the πρεσβύτεραι here are simply 'older women'.

A roll-call of Paul's co-workers – Romans 16.1–16

One further Pauline passage remains to be considered in our search for incidental evidence about the role of women in the Pauline churches. At the end of the letter to the Romans Paul appends an unusually long list of greetings to individuals in the Roman church, together with a commendation of one Phoebe, who probably took the letter to Rome from Corinth, where Paul wrote it. The length of the list is remarkable in view of the fact that Paul had not yet been to Rome.[6] Presumably these were people

---

5 K.E. Bailey, *Anvil* 11 (1994) 13–15. He quotes in support L. Swidler, *Biblical Affirmations of Women* (Philadelphia: Westminster, 1979), 315.

6 This has been one of the reasons why some have argued that 16.1–23 was originally a separate letter, probably to a different church where Paul had himself worked, e.g. Ephesus. (Lietzmann's famous response that such a letter 'may be intelligible in the age of the picture postcard; for any earlier period it is a monstrosity' provoked an equally acid reply from J.I.H. McDonald, *NTS* 16 [1969–70], 372: 'What kind of postcards did Lietzmann write?'.) See C.E.B. Cranfield's full study of the question, *The Epistle to the Romans*, vol. 1 (ICC.

with whom he had been associated in his itinerant work in other parts of the empire whom he now knew to have moved to Rome. Prisca and Aquila are a case in point: they were originally from Rome (Acts 18.2), and after their stay in Corinth and Ephesus had now apparently been able to return home.

Romans 16:1–16 mentions twenty-seven individuals, as well as conveying general greetings to the households of Aristobulus and of Narcissus. It is a remarkable confirmation of the significant role played by women in the New Testament churches that ten of the twenty-seven people greeted are women (not to mention the female members of the two households). Two of these women are merely mentioned without any further information (Julia, and the sister of Nereus, v. 15), but in the eight other cases Paul has more to say about their role.

Rufus' mother (v. 13) is described as a mother to Paul also, a mark probably of her seniority and supportive role, but not of a specifically ministerial function.

Mary (v. 6) has 'worked very hard among you'; Tryphaena and Tryphosa are 'workers in the Lord' (v. 12), and Persis also 'has worked hard in the Lord' (v. 12). The contribution of all four of these women is described by the same verb, κοπιάω, a strong term for 'toil' or 'labour' often with the connotation of resulting exhaustion (Mt. 11.28; Jn. 4.6). Paul uses the same verb elsewhere to describe not only his manual occupation (1 Cor. 4.12) but also his own apostolic labours (1 Cor. 15.10; Gal. 4.11; Phil. 2.16, etc.) as well as the Christian ministry of his associates (1 Cor. 16.16; 1 Thes. 5.12). That the 'labour' of these women was in specifically Christian ministry is indicated by the addition of ἐν κυρίῳ ('in the Lord') twice in v. 12, and Mary's labour εἰς ὑμᾶς ('among you' or 'for your benefit', v. 6) suggests a recognised role of ministry within the church. Paul's brief references do not allow us to be more specific than that.

He says a little more about Prisca (and, of course, Aquila!), whose role in Acts we have already considered. They are his συνεργοί ('co-workers') a term he uses for other associates with a central role in the Christian

Edinburgh: T & T Clark, 1975), 5–11, offering a satisfying explanation of the presence of such a list in a letter to Rome, and concluding, rightly in my view, that it is most likely that 'Paul wrote 1.1 – 16.23 to the church in Rome'.

mission, such as Timothy (Rom. 16.21), Titus (2 Cor. 8.23) and Epaphroditus (Phil. 2.25). Several other συνεϱγοί are named in Col. 4.10–11; Phm. 1,23–24, including such well-known names as Mark, Luke and Epaphras. That three women (Priscilla, Euodia and Syntyche, see above on Phil. 4:2-3) are among the named συνεϱγοί of Paul in the New Testament says much for the inclusion of women not only in the membership but in the active ministerial personnel of the apostolic churches. That Prisca's role was a far from merely nominal one is clear from Paul's comments on how she and Aquila have risked their necks and deserved the gratitude of all the Gentile churches (Rom. 16.4).

Then there is Junia,[7] who is apparently classed as an apostle (v. 7). This remarkable description for a woman has in modern times been evaded by the attempt to make her into a man. The Greek 'Ιουνιαν could be accented either as 'Ιουνίαν, making it the accusative of the common female name 'Ιουνία, or as 'Ιουνιᾶν, which would be the accusative of a masculine name 'Ιουνιᾶς. But no other instance of the masculine name Junias is known, and there seems little doubt that it would not have been suggested here but for the unwillingness of some in the Western church to accept that a woman could be described as 'prominent among the apostles'. There is no evidence of any text, version or commentary opting for the supposed masculine form of the name earlier than the late thirteenth century, and that was in the West; in the East the shift did not begin until the nineteenth century![8] Modern English versions are therefore rightly reverting to the form 'Junia' as used in the Authorised Version.[9] There really is no reason other than what Cranfield describes as 'mere conventional prejudice' for doubting that Junia was a woman.[10] As Kenneth Bailey comments, 'To insist on this

---

7 I am assuming the generally accepted reading 'Ιουνιαν rather than 'Ιουλιαν. The textual evidence is strongly in support of the former, and Julia is in any case mentioned separately in v. 15.

8 See K.E. Bailey, *Anvil* 11 (1994), 11–13.

9 So REB, NRSV, each reversing the decision of their predecessors. The forthcoming revised edition of the NIV will also restore the name Junia. For a detailed and decisive discussion see C.E.B. Cranfield, *Romans*, vol. 2, 788–789. Cf J.D.G. Dunn, *Romans 9–16* (Dallas: Word, 1988), 894–895.

10 The entry in BAGD is remarkable for its bias. They offer the masculine form 'Ιουνιᾶς, rightly described as 'not found elsewhere', followed by the grudging comment that 'The possibility, from a purely lexical point of view, that this is a

being a masculine name is like finding a text with the name Mary in it and arguing that it refers to a man. Such an argument is theoretically possible but would surely hinge on the finding of at least one text where Mary is clearly a male name.'[11]

Andronicus and Junia (assumed by ancient commentators to have been husband and wife) are described by Paul not only as his relatives and fellow-prisoners, and as having been 'in Christ before I was', but also as 'prominent among the apostles'. It is well-known that while Luke uses the term ἀπόστολος for the twelve, elsewhere in the New Testament it can be applied more widely. Indeed even Luke uses the term for Barnabas and Paul (Acts 14.4,14), and Paul, despite his impassioned defence of his own apostolic status, uses the term also of Apollos (probably, 1 Cor. 4.9), of Epaphroditus (Phil. 2.25), of himself, Silvanus and Timothy (1 Thes. 2.7) and of an unnamed group of 'envoys of the churches' (2 Cor. 8.23). It is in this company of travelling missionary leaders that Junia apparently finds her place. 'Apostle' in this sense is not so specific a term as when applied to the twelve, but it is undoubtedly a mark of high respect and significant responsibility within the leadership of the missionary church. In order to avoid the embarrassment of a female apostle it has been suggested that ἐπίσημοι ἐν τοῖς ἀποστόλοις might be translated 'highly-regarded *by* the apostles' rather than 'prominent among the apostles', but no English version that I have discovered has adopted this unnatural rendering.[12]

The remaining woman in Romans 16.1–16 is Phoebe, described as a διάκονος ('deacon') of the church in Cenchreae (vv. 1–2). The role of a διάκονος is not a defined one in the New Testament, and indeed may have been quite varied. Phoebe is the only woman to whom this

---

woman's name . . . deserves consideration'. They admit that this is the way the ancient commentators took it, but fail to point out also that, unlike the purely conjectural masculine form, the female name Junia was in common use.

11 *Anvil* 11 (1994), 12.

12 The New Jerusalem Bible (1985) renders the sense well by 'those outstanding apostles', but then unaccountably goes on to substitute for the name Junia the form 'Junius', for which there is no textual authority at all! The 1990 printing changes the name to 'Junias'.

title is specifically given. She was apparently a person of sufficient authority to be entrusted with taking Paul's letter to the Roman church. Paul's commendation of her to that church concludes with the intriguing description of her as προστάτις of many and of Paul himself as well. Προστάτης, and its feminine form προστάτις, derives from the verb προΐστημι, which can be used in the different senses of either 'be at the head of, rule, direct' or 'be concerned about, care for, give aid'; in two Pauline passages, Romans 12.8 and 1 Thessalonians 5.12, commentators and versions differ as to which sense is intended. On the basis of the second meaning of the verb, and in the light of the preceding request that they in their turn should provide help for Phoebe, προστάτις here has generally been understood to mean something like 'helper', 'supporter', 'a good friend', and the sense of leadership or authority has not been given any weight. But it is worth noting that the noun προστάτης, which is not used elsewhere in the New Testament, had by this time acquired a more technical sense as 'patron' or 'protector'. It is a word of social superiority and of authority. How much of this technical sense we can read into Paul's use of the feminine form is questionable, but it may well be that Phoebe was more than just a 'helper'. NRSV uses 'benefactor', which is closer to the secular usage, and Dunn argues strongly that the word should be allowed to carry 'its most natural and obvious sense of "patron" . . . (or alternatively "leader, ruler")'. He goes on to suggest concerning Phoebe's role as διάκονος, 'It may be that we should see the two roles as linked – "deacon" of the church because of her well-known patronage of "many" foreign visitors. . . . Paul was not the first leader of a new movement to benefit from the patronage of influential or wealthy women, and he certainly was not the last.'[13]

In Romans 16.1–16, therefore, we have a remarkable insight into the varied and influential role played by women in the Pauline churches, including not only the titles 'deacon' and 'apostle', but also a wider recognition that they, along with the men, had been in the forefront of the missionary work and leadership of the churches, as

---

13 J.D.G. Dunn, *Romans 9–16*, 888–889.

Paul's co-workers. This material, together with the evidence we have cited from other Pauline letters and from Acts, is in such striking contrast with the refusal in 1 Timothy 2.11–12 to allow a woman to teach or to have authority, and with the concept of 'submission', that it raises sharply the hermeneutical question of where within the varied and apparently conflicting testimony of the New Testament it is right to start to construct our biblical understanding of women's ministry. We shall return to that question shortly. First we must bring into the discussion Paul's famous statement in Galatians 3.28.

'No longer male and female'

When Paul wants to emphasise the universality of the gospel he is fond of using contrasting pairs to make his point: 'Jews or Greeks, slaves or free' (1 Cor. 12.13); 'Greek and Jew, circumcised and uncircumcised, barbarian, Scythian, slave and free' (Col. 3.11). In Galatians 3.28 we find a similar list to emphasise how we are 'all one in Christ Jesus', but this time the 'Jew or Greek, slave or free' are joined by 'no longer male and female'. The formulation of the final pair is different from those which precede: literally it reads 'There is not Jew nor Greek, there is not slave nor free, there is not male *and* female.' It is often suggested that the unexpected use of καί ('and') between the final pair is a deliberate echo of Genesis 1.27: 'male *and* female he created them' (where LXX uses the same terms ἄρσεν καὶ θῆλυ, 'male and female', rather than ἀνὴρ καὶ γυνή, 'man and woman'). But it is not so easy to see what such an echo would be intended to achieve. Genesis 1.26–30 offers no hint of inequality between the sexes; it is in Genesis 2 and 3 that this begins to emerge. To assert the equality of man and woman in Christ is not therefore in any way to question what Genesis 1.27 says, still less to suggest that Christ has in some way superseded the original creation. In Genesis 1, no less than in Galatians 3, man and woman are equal partners. What then is Paul denying by his phrase 'not male and female'?

Judging by the rest of his writings, he is certainly not asserting that there is now no difference between the sexes, that God is now substituting an androgynous

humanity for the sexual beings he originally created.[14]
Men and women in Paul's letters may be equal, but they
are certainly not the same! Some interpreters suggest
rather that while the nature of the marriage relationship is
not spelled out in Genesis 1, Paul's allusion to Genesis
1.27 is a short-hand way of evoking that relationship; his
point will then be that whereas hitherto woman's identity
has been understood in terms of her relationship to her
husband (i.e. she counts only as part of the 'male-*and*-
female' unit), in Christ she has her own significance,
whether married or not.[15] While I have little doubt that the
Paul who wrote 1 Corinthians 7 would agree heartily with
this view in itself, it seems to me that to allude to Genesis
1.27 rather than to a text which sets out the nature of the
marriage relationship would be an odd way to express it. I
conclude therefore that while Paul's wording here echoes
Genesis 1.27 (whether consciously or not), he is making
his point in its own right rather than by contrast with the
Old Testament text.

In context his concern is with the equality before God of
all who have been baptised into Christ; there are no
second-class citizens in the kingdom of God. In so far as
human society since the fall (and particularly Jewish
society)[16] has treated women as 'less equal' than men in
their membership of the people of God, it has fallen short
of God's ideal which now in Christ is being implemented.
Unfortunately for our present purpose, it is not part of
Paul's agenda at this point in his letter to work out the
implications of this basic insight for the respective roles of
men and women in different areas of life, and particularly
in Christian worship and ministry, and the implications
drawn by commentators tend to be heavily influenced by

---

14 This bizarre idea, espoused by some modern interpreters, owes nothing to
either Genesis or Paul, but everything to later gnostic speculation. See, briefly,
F.F. Bruce, *Commentary on Galatians* (Exeter: Paternoster, 1982), 189.

15 This suggestion features prominently in the detailed studies of Galatians 3.28
by Ben Witherington III in *NTS* 27 (1981) 593–604 and by K.R. Snodgrass in A.
Mickelsen (ed.), *Women, Authority and the Bible*, 161–181.

16 Commentators generally understand the three elements of Gal. 3.28 as a
deliberate counterpart to the male prayer of thanksgiving in the synagogue that
God did not create him a Gentile, a woman or an illiterate (see above). That
prayer has remained part of authorised Jewish worship into the twentieth
century.

their own presuppositions. It is certainly not true that he is here pronouncing specifically for or against the ordination of women, but it is equally unlikely that he would have regarded this formula as having no relevance at all to such an issue.

Perhaps the most we can safely say is that Paul here expresses the end-point of the historical trajectory which we have been tracing in this lecture, from the male-dominated society of the Old Testament and of later Judaism, through the revolutionary implications and yet still limited actual outworking of Jesus' attitude to women, and on to the increasing prominence of women in the apostolic church and in its active ministry. At all points within the period of biblical history the working out of the fundamental equality expressed in Galatians 3.28 remained constrained by the realities of the time, and yet increasingly the church was discovering that in Christ there was the basis, indeed the imperative, for the dismantling of the sexual discrimination which had prevailed since the fall. How far along that trajectory it is appropriate and possible for the church to move at any subsequent stage in history must remain a matter for debate, as it is today. But the witness of the New Testament challenges us to question any aspect of our common life in Christ which does not give appropriate expression for our day and social context to the fundamental principle that there is 'no longer male and female'.

Opposing views, and changing minds

Our brief survey of the wider biblical context must conclude. It is time to return to the issue from which we began and to attempt some conclusions.

We asked how evangelicals with an equal concern to be faithful to Scripture could come to opposite conclusions on the ordination of women. I hope that this book has at least illustrated how it is possible for either side to offer impressive biblical backing for their view.

Those opposed to women's ordination can appeal both to the general principle of the submission of women to men, and to a number of specific texts which appear to rule decisively against women exercising the sort of functions which are involved in ordained ministry. In response, those on the other side may question how relevant the question of submission within the marriage relationship is to ministry in the church, and may point to the many exegetical problems involved in the key 'prohibition' texts (and the uncertain textual status of one of them), quite apart from the issue of whether the rulings required by certain specific problems in two first-century churches can properly be understood as intended to apply to all churches in all circumstances, now as well as then.

Those in favour of women's ordination will appeal to a broader scriptural canvas, tracing the trajectory towards equality between men and women which we have outlined in this chapter, and pointing out the extent of the evidence within the New Testament itself that women were in fact already exercising functions in the church which do not easily square with a universal application of the 'prohibition' texts, and that they were doing so with the evident approval even of Paul, the author of those texts. In response, those on the other side may point out the still limited nature of such ministry by women in the New Testament, the all-male composition of the twelve, and the fact that the principle of the man being 'head' of the woman is applied by Paul not only to the marriage relationship but also in 1 Corinthians 11.3 apparently to the respective roles of men and women in worship.

Must we then settle for a stale-mate? Neither side will allow that their own case is less than compelling, but neither appears able to convince the other. I certainly do not imagine that such a dead-lock can be easily broken. But I think that some hope for movement may be derived from the fact that the position has not in fact remained static over the last two or three decades. Quite a lot of evangelicals have changed their minds. The movement, as far as I am aware, has been largely in one direction, in that there are now many more evangelicals within the Church of England who favour women's ordination than would have been the case even twenty years ago, while I am not aware of any who have moved from a position of support or neutrality to one of opposition. What then has been the cause of this movement?

Those who remain opposed to women's ordination would attribute it to an unwillingness to stand up against the tide of opinion both in society at large and within the Church of England (or at least among its leadership). It is certainly possible for Christians (even evangelical Christians!) to be swayed, even unconsciously, by the secular agenda, and by a desire not to appear negative and obstructive within a church dominated by a 'liberal' agenda. Such capitulation to the ways of the world may even be justified on the grounds of evangelistic necessity – no-one can be expected to listen to a gospel preached by a church whose very structures deny one of the fundamental values of the twentieth century, that of the equality of the sexes. Given such an analysis of the situation, it is natural for other evangelicals to dig in more deeply to defend the distinctive values of biblical Christianity, and to deplore the 'defection' of their fellow-evangelicals as unfaithfulness to the revealed will of God in Scripture.

But I hope our study has indicated that there may be other and more honourable reasons for evangelicals to have changed their minds on this issue. Those reasons are not political but hermeneutical. They, no less than those who maintain the traditional stance, believe that their view is a matter of truth rather than of expediency. If this is a valid claim (and I have made no attempt in this book to hide my belief that it is), then I believe that this issue does in fact offer us, as I suggested at the beginning, a valuable 'test-case in biblical hermeneutics', with a relevance to those many other issues on which evangelical Christians are similarly divided. Let me, in conclusion, attempt to spell this out in more general terms (without attempting to repeat or even to summarise all the ground we have covered).

Being faithful to the text – which text, and what is faithfulness?

We have seen that fundamental to this issue has been the question of which among differing biblical texts or themes is considered to be basic. The existence of competing emphases in Scripture is a common feature of our areas of disagreement – otherwise, I hope, we should not be able to disagree! Once we choose to begin at a given point, everything else will be viewed and interpreted in the light of that starting-point. F.F. Bruce expresses the situation very clearly in his comment on Galatians 3.28: 'Paul states the basic principle here; if restrictions on it are found elsewhere in the Pauline corpus, as in 1 Cor. 14.34f. . . . or 1 Tim. 2.11f., they are to be understood in relation to Gal. 3.28, and not *vice versa*.'[17] Once such a decision has been made, the conclusion is inevitable. But how did Bruce conclude that this principle rather than that of 1 Timothy 2.11–12 is 'basic'?

There is no rule of thumb – that is precisely our problem. A judgement has to be made, and not all will make it in the same way. Probably we all have our 'canon within the canon' (by which we mean those parts of Scripture with which we feel comfortable, and which say what we would like them to say) which we regard as 'basic'. But those instinctive preferences are normally derived from the tradition within which we have been brought up, rather than from an informed and principled choice made on the basis of the texts themselves.

When people change their minds on such an issue it is because something has caused them to question their inherited tradition. That 'something' may be a pure intellectual argument, but it is much more likely to be a newly-discovered current of thought or experience, not necessarily within Christian circles. The questions raised by secular society may quite properly cause us to re-examine our assumptions, and may lead us to place our emphasis on hitherto neglected aspects of the biblical revelation.

That is what has happened over the ordination of women. Many of us were brought up to assume that Paul's 'prohibition' texts were basic on this issue; here after all were specific apostolic injunctions apparently directly applicable to the issue. But exposure to the current debate has opened our eyes to the wider pattern of biblical revelation which I have attempted to sketch in this chapter, and this discovery has opened up the possibility to find our 'basic' position, with Bruce, not in these few texts but in a trajectory of thought and practice developing through Scripture, and arguably pointing beyond itself to the fuller outworking of God's ultimate purpose in Christ

---

17 F.F. Bruce, *Galatians*, 190.

in ways which the first-century situation did not yet allow. If this understanding of the essential equality of man and woman and this biblical recognition of an appropriate role for women in the authoritative and teaching ministry of the church is taken as 'basic', then it is inevitable that a question-mark is placed against the universal applicability of those texts which we formerly took as our starting-point.

And that leads us to the other main issue high-lighted by this 'test-case'. What does it mean to be 'faithful' to Scripture? Does it mean to regard every text as on a level, and all as permanently and literally applicable to all Christians in all circumstances? When the question is put like that the answer is obvious, and yet some of our traditional uses of Scripture come close to such a view. Yet within the Bible itself we see the applicability of texts changing. When Jesus illustrates in Matthew 5 what it means to 'fulfil' the law and the prophets he lays to rest any idea that the function of the law could continue unchanged in the age of fulfilment, and we have not been slow to learn the lesson that many of the laws which Old Testament Israel was expected to observe literally (most obviously, but not only, the sacrificial laws) no longer apply in the same way. Within the New Testament we find rules laid down which we seem to have found no difficulty in setting aside from the point of view of literal observance (e.g. the prohibition of 'eating blood' in Acts 15.29; the covering of women's heads at worship, 1 Cor. 11.2–16; the rules for the care of widows in 1 Timothy 5). We cannot therefore simply assume that a given rule for the New Testament churches will necessarily apply in the same way to us today; the issue needs to be discussed. And in that discussion the bearing of the total witness of Scripture on the issue must play a central role. In this final chapter I have tried to offer such an overview, and for me at least it points decisively away from the traditional understanding of the contemporary relevance of Paul's prohibition texts.

No doubt there are many other hermeneutical lessons to be learned from our study, which may also be found to have a wider application than merely to the issue of the ordination of women. But I hope that these rather sketchy remarks have been enough at least to explain to those who take a different position on this issue why some of us have found it necessary to change our minds, not in despite of the witness of Scripture but precisely in order to be faithful to it. If they can even help to lead others along the same road, I shall of course be the better pleased!